the Vampire Diaries

Stefan's Diaries

Also by L.J. Smith

THE VAMPIRE DIARIES NOVELS
Volume 1 (books 1 & 2) – The Struggle/The Awakening
Volume 2 (books 3 & 4) – The Fury/The Reunion
Book 5: The Return – Nightfall
Book 6: The Return – Shadow Souls
Book 7: The Return – Midnight
Book 8: The Hunters – Phantom
Book 9: The Hunters – Moonsong
Book 10: The Hunter – Destiny Rising

THE NIGHT WORLD NOVELS
Volume 1: Secret Vampire/Daughters of Darkness/
Enchantress
Volume 2: Dark Angel/The Chosen/Soulmate
Volume 3: Huntress/Black Dawn/Witchlight

THE STEFAN'S DIARIES NOVELS
Book 1: Origins
Book 2: Bloodlust
Book 3: The Craving
Book 4: The Ripper
Book 5: The Asylum
Book 6: The Compelled

THE NIGHT WORLD NOVELS
Volume 1: Secret Vampire/Daughters of Darkness/
Enchantress
Volume 2: Dark Angel/The Chosen/Soulmate
Volume 3: Huntress/Black Dawn/Witchlight

THE SECRET CIRCLE NOVELS
Volume 1: The Initiation and The Captive part I
Volume 2: The Captive part II and The Power
Book 3: The Divide

the Vampire Diaries

Stefan's Diaries

volume two

BLOODLUST

Based on the novels by

L. J. SMITH

and the TV series developed by
Kevin Williamson and Julie Plec

Hodder Children's Books

A division of Hachette Children's Books

First published in the USA in 2011 by
HarperTeen, an imprint of HarperCollins Publishers

This edition published in Great Britain in 2011
by Hodder & Stoughton

4

ISBN-13: 978 1 444 96825 5

Typeset in Berkeley by Avon DataSet Ltd,
Bidford on Avon, Warwickshire

Printed and bound in Great Britain by
Clays Ltd, Elcograf S.p.A.

The paper and board used in this paperback by Hodder Children's Books are natural recyclable products made from wood grown in sustainable forests. The manufacturing processes conform to the environmental regulations of the country of origin.

Hodder Children's Books
An imprint of
Hachette Children's Group
Part of Hodder & Stoughton
Carmelite House
50 Victoria Embankment
London EC4Y 0DZ

An Hachette UK company
www.hachette.co.uk

www.hachettechildrens.co.uk

'Tis now the very witching time of night,
When churchyards yawn and hell itself breathes out
Contagion to this world. Now could I drink hot blood
And so such bitter business as the day
Would quake to look on.

Hamlet, William Shakespeare

PREFACE

The poets and philosophers I once loved had it wrong. Death does not come to us all, nor does the passage of time dim our memories and reduce our bodies to dust. Because while I was considered dead, and a headstone had been engraved with my name, in truth my life was just beginning. It was as if I'd been asleep these many years, slumbering in the darkest night, only to awake to a world that was brighter, wilder, more thrilling than I'd ever imagined.

The humans I used to know continued their lives, just as I once had, spending their finite days going to the market, tending the fields, stealing secret kisses when the sun went down. They were merely shadows to me now, no more significant than the frightened squirrels and rabbits that scampered in the forest, barely conscious of the world around them.

But I was no shadow. I was whole – and impervious to their worst fear. I had conquered death. I was no fleeting visitor to the world. I was its master, and I had all of eternity to bend it to my will . . .

CHAPTER 1

It was October. The trees of the cemetery had turned a decayed brown, and a cold breeze had whistled in, replacing the stifling heat of the Virginia summer. Not that I much felt it. As a vampire, my body registered only the temperature of my next victim, warmed by the anticipation of her hot blood coiling through my veins.

My next victim was only a few feet away: a chestnut-haired girl who was currently climbing over the fence of the Hartnett estate, which ran adjacent to the cemetery.

'Clementine Haverford, whatever are you doing out of bed so late?' My playful demeanour was at odds with the hot, heavy thirst coursing through me. Clementine was not supposed to be here, but Matt Hartnett had always been sweet on her. And even though Clementine was engaged to Randall Haverford, her Charleston-based cousin, it was clear the feeling was mutual. She was already playing a dangerous game. Little did she know it was about to turn deadly.

Clementine squinted into the darkness. I could tell from her heavy-lidded expression and wine-stained teeth that she'd had a long night. 'Stefan Salvatore?' she gasped. 'But you're dead.'

I took a step closer to her. 'Am I now?'

'Yes, I attended your funeral.' She cocked her head to the side. She didn't seem too concerned, though. She was practically sleepwalking, heady from sips of wine and stolen kisses. 'Are you a dream?'

'No, not a dream,' I said huskily.

I grasped her by the shoulders and pulled her close to me. She fell against my chest, and the loud drum of her heartbeat filled my ears. She smelled of jasmine, just as she had last summer when my hand had grazed the bodice of her dress while we played one of Damon's kissing games under the Wickery Bridge.

I ran one finger along her cheek. Clementine had been my first crush, and I'd often wondered what it would feel like to hold her like this. I put my lips to her ear. 'I'm more like a nightmare.'

Before she could make a sound, I sank my teeth straight into her jugular vein, sighing when the first stream hit my mouth. Unlike what her name might suggest, Clementine's blood wasn't nearly as sweet as I'd imagined. Instead it tasted smoky and bitter, like coffee burned over a hot stove. Still, I drank deeply, gulping her down, until she stopped groaning and her pulse slowed to a whisper. She went limp in my arms, and the fire that burned in my veins and my belly was quenched.

All week I'd been hunting at my leisure, having discovered that my body required two feedings a day. Mostly I just listened to the vital fluid coursing through the bodies of the residents of Mystic Falls, fascinated by how easily I could take it from them. When I had attacked, I'd done so carefully, feeding on guests at the boarding house or taking one of the soldiers up by Leestown. Clementine would be my first victim who'd once been a friend – the first victim the people of Mystic Falls would miss.

Disengaging my teeth from her neck, I licked my lips, allowing my tongue to savour the spot of wet blood at the corner of my mouth. Then I dragged her out of the cemetery and back to the quarry where my brother, Damon, and I had been staying since we'd been turned.

The sun was just creeping over the horizon, and Damon was sitting listlessly at the edge of the water, glancing into its depths as if they held the secret to the universe. He'd been like that every day since we'd woken up as vampires seven days earlier, mourning the loss of Katherine, the vampire who'd made us into what we are now. Though she had turned me into a powerful creature, I celebrated her death, unlike my brother. She had played me for a fool, and the memory of her reminded me of how vulnerable I'd once been.

As I watched Damon, Clementine moaned in my arms, one eye fluttering open. Were it not for the blood seeping onto the blue lace neckline of her wrinkled, blue tulle dress, it would seem as if she were merely in slumber.

'Shhh,' I murmured, tucking a few loose strands of hair behind her ear. A voice somewhere in my mind told me that I should feel regret over taking her life, but I felt nothing at all. Instead, I readjusted her in my arms, tossing her over my shoulder, as if she were simply a sack of oats, and walked to the edge of the water.

'Brother.' I unceremoniously dumped Clementine's nearly lifeless body at his feet.

Damon shook his head and said, 'No.' His lips had a chalky white texture. Blood vessels twisted darkly on his face; they looked like cracks in marble. In the weak morning light, he looked like one of the broken statues in the cemetery.

'You must drink!' I said roughly, pushing him down, surprised at my own strength. His nostrils flared. But just as it was to mine, the smell of her blood was intoxicating to his weary body, and soon his lips met her skin in spite of his protestations. He began to drink, slowly at first, then lapped up the liquid as though he were a horse desperate for water.

'Why do you keep making me do this?' he asked plaintively, wiping his mouth with the back of his hand and wincing.

'You need to regain your strength.' I prodded Clementine with the tip of my dirt-caked boot. She groaned softly, somehow still alive. For now, at least. But her life was in my hands. The realization trilled through me, as though my entire being were on fire. This – the hunt, the conquests, the reward of the pleasurable sleepiness that always followed a feeding – made eternity stand before us as an endless adventure. Why couldn't Damon understand?

'This isn't strength. It's weakness,' Damon hissed, rising to his feet. 'It's hell on Earth, and nothing could be worse.'

'Nothing? Would you rather be dead, like Father?' I shook my head incredulously. 'You have a second chance.'

'I never asked for it,' Damon said sharply. 'I never asked for any of this. All I wanted was *Katherine*. She's gone, so kill me now and be done with it.' Damon handed me a jagged oak branch. 'Here,' he said, standing with his arms open wide, his chest exposed. Just one stroke to his heart and he'd have his wish.

Memories flashed through my mind: of Katherine, her soft, dark curls, her fangs bright in the moonlight, her head arched back before she bit into my neck, her ever-present lapis lazuli pendant that sat in the hollow of her neck. I now understood why she'd killed my fiancée, Rosalyn, why she'd compelled me and Damon, why she used her beauty and innocent visage to make people want to trust and protect her. It was her nature. And now it was ours. But instead of accepting it as a gift, as I had, Damon seemed to think it was a curse.

I cracked the branch over my knee and threw the shards into the river. 'No,' I said. Though I'd never admit it aloud, the thought of living forever without a friend in the world frightened me. I wanted Damon and I to learn to be vampires together.

'No?' Damon repeated, his eyes snapping open. 'You're man enough to murder an old flame, but not your brother?' He shoved me to the ground. He loomed above me, his own fangs bared, then spat on my neck.

'Don't embarrass yourself,' I said, scrambling to my feet. He was strong, but I was far stronger, thanks to my regular feedings. 'And don't fool yourself into thinking Katherine loved you,' I growled. 'She loved her Power, and she loved what she could make us do for her. But she never loved us.'

Damon's eyes blazed. He rushed towards me with the speed of a galloping horse. His shoulder, hard as stone, ploughed into me, throwing me back into a tree. The trunk split with a loud crack. 'She loved *me*.'

'Then why did she turn me, too?' I challenged, rolling to my feet as I rebuffed his next blow.

The words had their desired effect. Damon's shoulders sagged, and he staggered backward. 'Fine. I'll just do it myself,' he murmured, grabbing another stick and running the sharp end along his chest.

I slapped the stake out of his hand and twisted his arms behind his back. 'You are my brother – my flesh and blood. So long as I stay alive, so shall you. Now, come.' I pushed him towards the woods.

'Come where?' Damon asked listlessly, allowing me to drag him along.

'To the cemetery,' I answered. 'We have a funeral to attend.'

Damon's eyes registered a dull spark of interest. 'Whose?'

'Father's. Don't you want to say goodbye to the man who killed us?'

CHAPTER 2

Damon and I crouched in the cemetery's hemlock grove behind the mausoleums that housed the bones of Mystic Falls' founders. Despite the early hour, already the townspeople stood stoop-shouldered around a gaping hole in the ground. Puffs of air curled into the cerulean blue sky with the crowd's every exhalation, as if the entire congregation were smoking celebratory cigars rather than trying to calm their chattering teeth.

My heightened senses took in the scene before us. The cloying smell of vervain – a herb that rendered vampires powerless – hung heavy in the air. The grass was laden with dew, each drop of water falling to the earth with a silvery ping, and far off in the distance church bells chimed. Even from this distance, I could see a tear lodged in the corner of Honoria Fells's eye.

Down at the pulpit, Mayor Lockwood shuffled from

foot to foot, clearly eager to get the crowd's attention. I could just make out the winged figure above him, the angel statue that marked my mother's final resting place. Two empty plots lay just beyond, where Damon and I should have been buried.

The mayor's voice sliced through the cold air, his voice as loud to my sensitive ears as if he were standing right next to me. 'We come together today to say farewell to one of Mystic Falls' greatest sons, Giuseppe Salvatore, a man for whom town and family always came before self.'

Damon kicked the ground. 'The family he killed. The love he destroyed, the lives he shattered,' he muttered.

'Shhh,' I whispered as I pressed my palm against his forearm.

'If I were to paint a portrait of this great man's life,' Lockwood continued over the sniffles and sighs of the crowd, 'Giuseppe Salvatore would be flanked by his two fallen sons, Damon and Stefan, heroes of the battle of Willow Creek. May we learn from Giuseppe, emulate him, and be inspired to rid our town of evil, either seen or unseen.'

Damon let out a low, rattling scoff. 'The portrait he paints,' he said, 'should contain the muzzle flash of Father's rifle.' He rubbed the place where Father's bullet had ripped through his chest only a week earlier. There was no physical wound – our transformation healed all injuries – but the betrayal would be etched in our minds forever. 'Shhh,' I said again as Jonathan Gilbert strode up to stand beside Mayor Lockwood, holding a large veiled frame. Jonathan looked to have aged ten years in seven short days: lines creased his tanned forehead, and streaks of white were visible in his brown hair. I wondered if his transformation had something to do with Pearl, the vampire he loved but had condemned to death after finding out what she really was.

I spotted Clementine's parents in the crowd, arms clasped, not yet aware that their daughter was not among the sombre-faced girls in the back of the crowd.

They'd find out soon enough.

My thoughts were interrupted by an insistent clicking, like a watch counting or a fingernail tapping against a hard surface. I scanned the crowd, trying to trace the ticking to its point of origin. The sound was slow and steady and mechanical, steadier than a heartbeat, slower than a metronome. And it seemed to be coming directly from Jonathan's hand. Clementine's blood rushed to my head.

The compass.

Back when Father first became suspicious of vampires, he'd created a committee of men to rid the town of the demonic scourge. I'd attended the meetings, which had taken place in Jonathan Gilbert's attic. He'd had plans for a contraption to identify vampires, and I'd witnessed him using it in action the week before. It was how he'd discovered Pearl's true nature.

I elbowed Damon. 'We have to go,' I said, barely moving my jaw.

Just then Jonathan looked up, and his eyes locked directly onto mine.

He let out an unholy shriek and pointed to our mausoleum. 'Demon!'

The crowd turned towards us as one, their stares cutting through the fog like bayonets. Then something rushed past me, and the wall behind me exploded. A cloud of powder billowed around us, and chips of marble slashed across my cheek.

I bared my fangs and roared. The sound was loud, primal, terrifying. Half the crowd knocked over chairs in their haste to flee the cemetery, but the other half remained.

'Kill the demons!' Jonathan cried, brandishing a crossbow.

'I think they mean us, brother,' Damon said with a short, humourless laugh.

And so I grabbed Damon and ran.

CHAPTER 3

With Damon behind me, I raced through the forest, jumping over felled branches and skipping over stones. I leaped over the waist-high iron gate of the cemetery, turning briefly to make sure Damon was still following. We zigzagged deep into the woods, the gunshots sounding like fireworks in my ear, the shrieks of the townspeople like breaking glass, their heavy breathing like low-rolling thunder. I could even hear the footfalls of the crowd pursuing me, each step sending vibrations through the ground. I silently cursed Damon for being so stubborn. If he'd been willing to drink before today, he'd be at full strength, and our newfound speed and agility would have already taken us far away from this mess.

As we cut through the thicket, squirrels and voles scattered from the underbrush, their blood quickening in the presence of predators. A whinny and a snort sounded from the far edge of the cemetery.

'Come *on*.' I grabbed Damon by the waist and hoisted him to his feet again. 'We have to keep moving.' I could hear the blood pumping, smell the iron, feel the ground shaking. I knew the mob was more afraid of me than I of them; but still, the sound of gunshots caused my mind to whirl, my body to lurch forward. Damon was weak and I could only carry him so far.

Another gunshot cracked, closer this time. Damon stiffened.

'Demons!' Jonathan Gilbert's voice sliced through the woods. Another bullet whizzed past me, grazing my shoulder. Damon flopped forward in my arms.

'Damon!' The word echoed in my ears, sounding so much like the word *demon* that it startled me. 'Brother!' I shook him, then began awkwardly dragging him behind me again towards the sounds of the horses. But despite having just fed, my strength wouldn't last forever, and the footsteps were coming closer and closer.

Finally we reached the edge of the cemetery, where several horses were tied to the iron hitching posts. They pawed at the ground, pulling on the ropes that tethered them so hard that their necks bulged. One coal-black mare was none other than my old horse, Mezzanotte. I stared at her, mesmerized at how desperate she appeared to be to get away from me. Just a few days earlier, I was the only rider she'd trusted.

Footfalls sounded again. I tore my gaze away, shaking my head at being so sentimental. I pulled Father's old hunting knife from the top of my boot. It had been the one thing I'd taken when I'd walked through Veritas, our family estate, one last time. He'd always had it with him, although I'd never seen him use it. Father had never been one to work with his hands. Still, in my mind's eye, the knife conveyed the power and authority that everyone had associated with my father.

I put the blade to the rope that tied Mezzanotte, but it didn't make even the smallest cut. Looking down, I saw the knife for what it was: a dull blade that could barely cut through twine, polished to look important. It was well suited to Father, I thought in disgust, throwing the knife to the ground and yanking at the ropes with my bare hands. The footsteps came closer and I looked wildly behind me. I had wanted to free all the horses so Jonathan and his men couldn't ride them, but there simply wasn't time.

'Hey, girl,' I murmured, stroking Mezzanotte's elegant neck. She pawed the ground nervously, her heart pounding. 'It's me,' I whispered as I swung myself onto her back. She reared up, and out of surprise, I kicked her so hard in the flanks that I heard the snap of a rib breaking. Instantly, she yielded in submission, and I trotted her to Damon.

'Come on,' I yelled.

A flicker of doubt passed across Damon's eyes, but then he reached over Mezzanotte's broad back and hoisted himself up. Whether it was fear or instinct, his willingness to flee gave me hope that he was not resolved to die, after all.

'Kill them!' a voice yelled, and someone threw a burning torch towards us that arced and landed on the grass at Mezzanotte's feet. Instantly, the grass began to burn, and Mezzanotte bolted in the opposite direction of the quarry. Hooves thudded behind us – the men had leaped on the other horses and were now fast on our tail.

Another gunshot rang out behind us, followed by the twang of a bow. Mezzanotte reared up, letting out a high whinny. Damon slipped, grappling to hold on to the underside of Mezzanotte's neck, while I tugged at the leather straps, trying to keep us upright. Only after a few steps backward did all four of Mezzanotte's hooves get back on the dirt. As Damon righted himself, I saw a slim wooden arrow jutting out from the horse's haunches. It was a clever tactic. At a distance, the mob had a far better chance of slowing down our horse than of striking one of us straight through the heart.

Hunched low over Mezzanotte, we galloped under branches and pressed on. She was a strong horse, but she favoured her left side, where the arrow had gone in. A wet streak of my own blood was streaming down my temple and onto my shirt, and Damon's grip on my waist was dangerously loose.

Still, I urged Mezzanotte forward. I was relying on instinct, on something beyond thinking and planning. It was as if I could smell freedom and possibility, and just had to trust that I'd lead us to it. I pulled the reins and steered out of the woods and into the field behind Veritas Estate.

On any other rainy morning there would have been lights in the window of our old home, the lamps giving the bubbled glass an orange-yellow look of sunset. Our maid, Cordelia, would have been singing in the kitchen, and Father's driver, Alfred, would be sitting sentry by the entrance. Father and I would be sitting in companionable silence in the breakfast room. Now the estate was a cold shell of its former self: the windows dark, the grounds completely silent. It had only been empty for a week, yet Veritas looked as though it had been abandoned for ages.

We leaped over the fence and landed unsteadily. I just barely managed to right us with a hard tug on the reins, the metal of the bit clacking against Mezzanotte's teeth. Then we thundered around the side of the house, my skin clammy as we passed Cordelia's plot of vervain, the tiny stalks ankle-high.

'Where are you taking us, brother?' Damon asked.

I heard three sets of splashing hooves as Jonathan Gilbert, Mayor Lockwood and Sheriff Forbes cut along the pond at the back of our property. Mezzanotte wheezed, a peach froth lining her mouth, and I knew that outriding them wouldn't be a possibility.

Suddenly, the throaty wail of a train whistled through the morning, blocking out the hooves, the wind, and the metallic rasp of a gun reloading.

'We're getting on that train,' I said, kicking Mezzanotte in the flanks. Bearing down, she picked up speed and sailed over the stone wall that separated Veritas from the main road.

'C'mon, girl,' I whispered. Her eyes were wild and terrified, but she ran faster down the road and onto Main Street. The charred church came into sight, blackened bricks rising up like teeth from the ashen earth. The apothecary had also been burned to the ground. Crucifixes were affixed to every single doorframe in town; vervain sprigs were hung in garlands over most. I barely recognized the place I'd lived all my seventeen years. Mystic Falls wasn't my home. Not anymore.

Behind us, Jonathan Gilbert and Mayor Lockwood's horses were approaching faster and faster. Ahead of us, I could hear the train drawing nearer, grinding against the rails. The froth at Mezzanotte's mouth was turning pink with blood. My fangs were dry, and I licked my parched lips, wondering if this constant desire for blood came with being a new vampire, or if I would always feel this way.

'Ready to go, brother?' I asked, yanking Mezzanotte's reins. She halted, giving me just enough time to jump off before she collapsed onto the ground, blood rushing from her mouth.

A shot rang out, and blood spurted from Mezzanotte's flank. I yanked Damon by the wrists and hurled us onto the caboose just before the train roared out of the station, leaving Jonathan Gilbert and Mayor Lockwood's angry cries far behind.

CHAPTER 4

The car was pitch black, but our eyes, now adapted for nocturnal vision, allowed us to pick out a path through the piles of sooty coal in the caboose. Finally we emerged through a doorway into what appeared to be a first-class sleeping car. When no one was looking, we stole a few shirts and pairs of trousers from an unattended trunk and put them on. They didn't fit perfectly, but they would do.

As we ventured out into the aisle of the seating coach, the train rumbling beneath our feet, a hand grabbed my shoulder. Reflexively, I swung my arm at my attacker and growled. A man in a conductor's uniform flew backward and hit the wall of a compartment with a *thud*.

I locked my jaw to keep my fangs from protruding. 'I'm sorry! You startled me and . . .' I trailed off. My voice was unfamiliar to my own ears. For the past week, most of my interactions had been in hoarse whispers. I was surprised at how human I sounded. But I was much more powerful than my voice betrayed. I hoisted the man to his feet and straightened his navy cap. 'Are you OK?'

'I believe so,' the conductor said in a dazed voice, patting his arms as if to make sure they were still there. He looked to be about twenty, with sallow skin and sandy hair. 'Your ticket?'

'Oh, yes, tickets,' Damon said, his voice smooth, not betraying that we had been in a gallop to the death only minutes before. 'My brother has those.'

I shot an angry glance towards him, and he smiled back at me, calm, taunting. I took him in. His boots were muddy and unlaced, his linen shirt was untucked from his trousers, but there was something about him – more than his aquiline nose and aristocratic jaw – that made him seem almost regal. In that moment, I barely recognized him: this wasn't the Damon I'd grown up with, or even the one I'd got to know in the past week. Now that we were hurtling out of Mystic Falls towards some invisible, unknowable point on the horizon, Damon had become someone else, someone serene and unpredictable. In these unfamiliar surroundings, I was unsure if we were partners in crime or sworn enemies.

The conductor turned his attention towards me, his lip curling as he took in my dishevelled appearance. I hastily tucked my own shirt in.

'We were rushing, and . . .' I drawled, hoping my Southern accent would make the words sound sincere – and human. His goldfish-like eyes bulged sceptically, and then I remembered a vampire skill Katherine had used on me to great effect: compelling. '. . . And I already showed you my ticket,' I said slowly, willing him to believe me.

The conductor furrowed his brows. 'No, you didn't,' he replied just as slowly, taking extra care to enunciate each word, as if I were an especially dull passenger.

I cursed silently, then leaned in ever closer. 'But I presented it to you earlier.' I stared into his eyes until my own started to cross.

The conductor took a step back and blinked. 'Everyone needs a ticket on their person at all times.'

My shoulders slumped. 'Well . . . uh . . .'

Damon stepped in front of me. 'Our tickets are in the sleeper car. Our mistake,' he said, his voice low and lulling. He didn't blink once as he gazed at the man's hooded lids.

The ticket taker's face went slack, and he took a step back. 'My mistake. Go ahead, gentlemen. I'm sorry about the confusion.' His voice was distant as he tipped his hat, then stood aside to let us walk into the gentlemen's club car.

As soon as the door shut behind us, I grabbed Damon's arm.

'How did you do that?' I asked. Had Katherine taught him how to drop his voice, gaze his victim in the eye, and force the poor lad to do his bidding? I clenched my jaw, wondering if she'd mentioned how easy it had been for her to compel me. Images flashed into my mind: Katherine widening her eyes, begging me to keep her secret, to stop my father from hunting her. I shook my head, as if to fling the images from my brain.

'Who's in charge now, brother?' Damon drawled, collapsing into an empty leather seat and yawning, his hands stretched above his head as if he were ready to settle down for a long nap.

'You're going to sleep now? Of all times?' I exclaimed.

'Why not?'

'Why not?' I repeated dumbly. I held out my arms, gesturing to our surroundings. We sat among well-dressed men in top hats and waistcoats, who, despite the hour, were busily patronizing the wood-panelled bar in the corner. A group of older men played poker, while young men in captain's uniforms whispered over tumblers of whiskey. We went unnoticed in this crowd. There were no vampire compasses revealing our true identities. No one so much as glanced in our direction as we sat down.

I perched on the ottoman opposite Damon. 'Don't you see?' I said. 'No one knows us here. This is our chance.'

'You're the one who doesn't see.' Damon inhaled deeply. 'Smell that?'

The warm, spicy scent of blood filled my nostrils, and the thud of pumping hearts echoed around me like cicadas on a summer evening. Instantly a searing pain ripped through my jaw. I covered my mouth with my hands, looking wildly around to see if anyone had noticed the long canines that had shot out from my gums.

Damon let out a wry chuckle. 'You'll never be free, brother. You're tethered to blood, to humans. They make you desperate and needy – they make you a killer.'

At the word *killer*, a man with a rust-coloured beard and sun-dyed cheeks glanced sharply at us from across the aisle. I forced a benign smile.

'*You're going to get us in trouble*,' I hissed under my breath.

'Yes, well, you've got only yourself to blame for that,' Damon replied. He closed his eyes, signalling the end of our conversation.

I sighed and glanced out the window. We were probably only thirty miles outside of Mystic Falls, but it felt as though everything I'd known before had simply ceased to exist. Even the weather was new – the rain shower had ended, and the autumn sun now poked through wispy clouds, penetrating the glass that separated the train from the outside world. It was curious: while our rings protected us from the sun searing our flesh, the burning orb made me feel slightly drowsy.

Pushing myself to stand, I took refuge in the dark aisles that led from compartment to compartment. I passed from walking between the plush velvet seats of the first-class cars to the wooden benches of second class.

Finally, I made myself comfortable in an empty sleeper cabin, drew the curtains, closed my eyes, and opened my ears.

Hope those Union boys get out of New Orleans and leave it to ourselves . . .

Once you see those beauties on Bourbon Street, your Virginia virgin won't look the same . . .

You've got to be careful. There's voodoo down there, and some say it's where demons come out to play . . .

I smiled. New Orleans sounded like the perfect place to call home.

I settled into the makeshift bed, content to relax and let the train rock me into some sort of slumber. I found that I fed much better after I had rested.

CHAPTER 5

A day later, the train screeched to a stop. 'Baton Rouge!' a conductor called in the distance.

We were getting closer to New Orleans, but the time was creeping by far too slowly for my liking. I flattened my back against the wall of the car, noticing passengers hastily packing up their belonging as they prepared to vacate their quarters, when my eye fell upon a green ticket, emblazoned with a large boot print. I knelt down and picked it up. *Mr Remy Picard, Richmond to New Orleans*.

I tucked it into my pocket and jauntily walked back through the train, until I felt someone gazing at me curiously. I turned around. Two sisters were smiling at me through the window of a private compartment, their expressions bemused. One was working on a piece of needlepoint, the other writing in a leather-bound diary. They were being watched with hawk-like intensity by a short, plump woman in her sixties, clad in all black, most likely their aunt or guardian.

I opened the door.

'Sir?' the woman said, turning towards me. I locked my gaze onto her watery blue eyes.

'I believe you left something in the dining car,' I said. 'Something you need,' I continued, copying Damon's low, steady voice. Her eyes shifted, but I sensed that this was different from the way the conductor had responded to my words. When I'd tried to compel the conductor, it was as if my thoughts had collided with steel; here, it was as though my thoughts were breaking through fog. She cocked her head, clearly listening.

'I left something . . .' She trailed off, sounding confused. But I could sense something in my brain, a sort of melding of our minds, and I knew she wouldn't fight me.

Immediately, the woman shifted her bulk and stood up from her seat.

'Why, ah, I believe I did,' she said, turning on her heel and walking back down the hall without a backward glance. The metallic door of the car closed with a click, and I pulled the heavy navy curtains over the little window to the aisle.

'Nice to make your acquaintance,' I said as I bowed to the two girls. 'My name is Remy Picard,' I said, surreptitiously gazing down at the ticket poking out of my breast pocket.

'Remy,' the taller girl repeated quietly, as if committing my name to memory. I felt my fangs throb against my gums. I was so hungry, and she was so exquisite . . . I mashed my lips together and forced myself to stand still. *Not yet*.

'Finally! Aunt Minnie's never left us alone!' the older girl said. She looked to be about sixteen. 'She thinks we aren't to be trusted.'

'Aren't you now?' I teased, easing into the flirtation as the compliments and responses volleyed back and forth. As a human, I would have hoped such an exchange would end with a squeeze of the hand or a brush of lips against a cheek. Now, all I could think of was the blood coursing through the girls' veins.

I sat down next to the older girl, the younger one's eyes searching me curiously. She smelled like gardenias and bread just out of the oven. Her sister – they must have been sisters, with the same tawny brown hair and darting blue eyes – smelled richer, like nutmeg and freshly fallen leaves. 'I'm Lavinia, and this is Sarah Jane. We're going to move to New Orleans,' the one girl said, putting her needlepoint down on her lap. 'Do you know it? I'm worried I'll miss Richmond horribly,' she said plaintively.

'Our papa died,' Sarah Jane added, her lower lip trembling.

I nodded, running my tongue along my teeth, feeling my

fangs. Lavinia's heart was beating far faster than her sister's.

'Aunt Minnie wants to marry me off. Will you tell me what's it like, Remy?' Lavinia pointed to the ring on my fourth finger. Little did she know that the ring had nothing to do with marriage and everything to do with being able to hunt girls like her in broad daylight.

'Being married is lovely, if you meet the right man. Do you think you'll meet the right man?' I asked, staring into her eyes.

'I . . . I don't know. I suppose if he's anything like you, then I should count myself lucky.' Her breath was hot on my cheek, and I knew that I couldn't control myself for much longer.

'Sarah Jane, I bet your auntie needs some help,' I said, glancing into Sarah Jane's blue eyes. She paused for a moment, then excused herself and went to find her aunt. I had no idea if I was compelling her or if she was simply following my orders, because she was a child and I was an adult.

'Oh, you're wicked, aren't you?' Lavinia asked, her eyes flashing as she smiled at me.

'Yes,' I said brusquely. 'Yes, I am wicked, my dear.' I bared my teeth, watching with great satisfaction as her eyes widened with horror. The best part of feeding was the anticipation, seeing my victim trembling, helpless, mine.

I slowly leaned in, savouring the moment. My lips grazed her soft skin.

'No!' she gasped.

'Shhh,' I whispered, pulling her closer and allowing my teeth to touch her skin, subtly at first, then more insistently, until I sank my teeth into her neck. Her moans became screams, and I held my hand over her mouth to silence her as I sucked the sweet liquid into my mouth. She groaned slightly, but soon her sighs turned into kittenish mews.

'New Orleans, next stop!' the conductor yelled, breaking my reverie.

I glanced out the window. The sun was sinking low into the sky, and Lavinia's nearly dead body felt heavy in my arms. Outside the window, New Orleans rose up as if in a dream, and I could see the ocean continuing on and on forever. It was like my life was destined to be: never-ending years, never-ending feedings, never-ending pretty girls with sweet sighs and sweeter blood.

'*Forever panting, and forever young,*' I whispered, pleased at how well the lines from the poet Keats suited my new life.

'Sir!' The conductor knocked on the door. I strode out of the compartment, wiping my mouth with the back of my hand. He was the same conductor who'd stopped Damon and me just outside Mystic Falls, and I saw suspicion flash across his face.

'We're in New Orleans, then?' I asked, the taste of Lavinia's blood in the back of my throat.

The ginger-haired conductor nodded. 'And the ladies? They're aware?'

'Oh yes, they're aware,' I said, not breaking my gaze as I slipped my ticket out of my pocket. 'But they asked not to be disturbed. And I ask not to be disturbed, too. You've never seen me. You've never been by this compartment. Later, if anyone asks, you say there may have been some thieves who got on the train outside Richmond. They looked suspicious. Union soldiers,' I invented.

'Union soldiers?' the conductor repeated, clearly confused.

I sighed. Until I had compelling under control, I'd have to resort to a more permanent style of memory erasing. In a flash I grabbed the conductor by the neck and snapped it as easily as if it were a sweet pea. Then I threw him into the compartment with Lavinia and shut the door behind me.

'Yes, Union soldiers always do make a bloody mess of things, don't they?' I asked rhetorically. Then, whistling the whole way, I went to collect Damon from the gentlemen's club car.

CHAPTER 6

Damon was slumped right where I'd left him, an untouched whiskey glass sweating on the oak table in front of him.

'Come on,' I said roughly, yanking him up by the arm.

The train was slowing, and all around us passengers were gathering their belongings and lining up behind a conductor who stood in front of the black iron doors to the outside world. But since we were unencumbered by possessions and blessed with strength, I knew our best bet was to exit the train the same way we'd entered: by jumping off the back of the caboose. I wanted us both to be long gone before anyone noticed anything was amiss.

'You look well, *brother*.' His tone was light, but the chalkiness of his skin and the purpling beneath his eyes gave away just how truly tired and hungry he was. For an instant, I wished I'd left some of Lavinia for him, but quickly brushed aside the thought. I had to take a firm hand. That was how Father used to train the horses. Denying them food until they finally stopped yanking on the reins and submitted to being ridden. It was the same with Damon. He needed to be broken.

'One of us has to maintain our strength,' I told Damon, my back to him as I led the way to the last car of the train.

The train was still creeping along, the wheels scraping against the iron lengths of track. We didn't have much time. We scrambled back through the sooty coal to the door, which I pulled open easily.

'On three! One . . . Two . . .' I grabbed his wrist and jumped. Both of our knees hit the hard dirt below with a thud.

'Always have to show off, don't you, brother?' Damon said, wincing. I noticed his trousers had been torn at the knees from the fall, and his hands were pockmarked with gravel. I was untouched, except for a scrape on my elbow.

'You should have fed.' I shrugged.

The whistle of the train shrieked, and I took in the sights. We were on the edge of New Orleans, a bustling city filled with smoke and an aroma like a combination of butter and firewood and murky water. It was far bigger than Richmond, which had been the largest city I'd ever known. But there was something else, a sense of danger that filled the air. I grinned. Here was a city we could disappear in.

I began walking towards town at the superhuman speed I still hadn't got used to, Damon trailing behind me, his footfalls loud and clumsy, but steady. We made our way down Garden Street, clearly a main artery of the city. Surrounding us were rows of homes, as neat and colourful as dollhouses. The air was soupy and humid, and voices speaking French, English, and languages I'd never heard created a patchwork of sound.

Left and right, I could see alleyways leading down to the water, and rows of vendors were set up on the sidewalks, selling everything from freshly caught turtles to precious stones imported from Africa. Even the presence of blue-coated Union soldiers on every street corner, their muskets at their hips, seemed somehow festive. It was a carnival in every sense of the word, the type of scene Damon would have loved when we were human. I turned to look over my shoulder. Sure enough, Damon's lips were curved in a slight smile, his eyes glowing in a way I hadn't seen in what felt like ages. We were in this adventure together, and now, away from memories of Katherine and Father's remains and Veritas, maybe Damon could finally accept and embrace who he was.

'Remember when we said we'd travel the world?' I asked, turning towards him. 'This is our world now.'

Damon nodded slightly. 'Katherine told me about New Orleans. She once lived here.'

'And if she were here, she'd want you to make this town your own – to live here, be here, to take your fill and make your place in the world.'

'Always the poet.' Damon smirked, but he continued to follow me.

'Perhaps, but it's true. All of this is ours,' I said encouragingly, spreading my hands wide.

Damon took a moment to consider my words and simply said, 'All right, then.'

'All right?' I repeated, hardly hoping to believe it. It was the first time he'd glanced into my eyes since our fight at the quarry.

'Yes. I'm following you.' He turned in a circle, pointing to the various buildings. 'So, where do we stay? What do we do? Show me this brave new world.' Damon's lips twisted into a smile, and I couldn't tell whether he was mocking me or was speaking in earnest. I chose to believe the latter.

I sniffed the air and immediately caught a whiff of lemon and ginger. *Katherine*. Damon's shoulders stiffened; he must have smelled it, too. Wordlessly, both of us spun on our heels and walked down an unmarked alleyway, following a woman wearing a satin lilac dress, a large sunbonnet on top of her dark curls.

'Ma'am!' I called.

She turned around. Her white cheeks were heavily rouged and her eyes ringed with kohl. She looked to be in her thirties, and already worry lines creased her fair forehead. Her hair fell in tendrils around her face, and her dress was cut low, revealing far too much of her freckled bosom than was strictly decorous. I knew instantly she was a scarlet woman, one we'd whisper about as boys and point to when we were in the tavern in Mystic Falls.

'You boys lookin' for a good time?' she said languidly, her gaze flicking from me to Damon, then back again. She wasn't Katherine, not even close, but I could see a flicker in Damon's eyes.

'*I don't think finding a place to stay will be a problem*,' I whispered under my breath.

'*Don't kill her*,' Damon whispered back, his jaw barely moving.

'Come with me. I have some gals who'd love to meet you. You seem like the type of boys who need adventure. That right?' She winked.

A storm was brewing, and I could vaguely hear thunderclaps in the far distance.

'We're always looking for an adventure with a pretty lady,' I said.

Out of the corner of my eye, I saw Damon tighten his jaw,

and I knew he was fighting the urge to feed. *Don't fight it*, I thought, fervently hoping Damon would drink as we followed her along the cobblestone streets.

'We're right here,' she said, using a large key to unlock the wrought-iron door of a periwinkle blue mansion at the end of a cul-de-sac. The house was well kept, but the buildings on either side seemed abandoned, with chipping paint and gardens overflowing with weeds. I could hear the jaunty sound of a piano playing within.

'It's my boarding house, Miss Molly's. Except, of course, at this boarding house we show you some *true* hospitality, if that's what you're in the mood for,' she said, batting her long eyelashes. 'Coming?'

'Yes, ma'am.' I pushed Damon through the doorway, then locked the door behind us.

CHAPTER 7

The next evening I gazed contented at the sun setting over the harbour. Miss Molly hadn't exaggerated: the girls at her house were hospitable. For breakfast I'd had one with long, corn-silk hair and bleary blue eyes. I could still taste her wine-laced blood on my lips.

Damon and I had spent the day wandering the city, taking in the wrought-iron balconies in the French Quarter – and the girls who waved to us from their perches there – the fine tailor shops with bolts of sumptuous silk in the windows, and the heady cigar shops where men with round bellies struck business deals.

But of all the sights, I liked the harbour best. This was the city's lifeblood, where tall ships carrying produce and exotic wares entered and exited. Cut off the harbour, you cut off the city, making it as vulnerable and helpless as Miss Molly's girl had been that morning.

Damon gazed out at the boats as well, rubbing his chin thoughtfully. His lapis lazuli ring glinted in the fading sunlight. 'I almost saved her.'

'Who?' I asked, turning sharply, hope swelling in my chest. 'Did you sneak off and feed from someone?'

My brother kept his eyes on the horizon. 'No, of course not. I meant Katherine.'

Of course. I sighed. If anything, last night had made Damon more malcontent than ever. While I'd enjoyed the company and the sweet blood of a girl whose name I would never know, Damon had retired to a room of his own, treating the establishment as if it were simply the boarding house it pretended to be.

'You should have drunk,' I said for the hundredth time that day. 'You should have taken your pick.'

'Don't you understand, Stefan?' Damon asked flatly. 'I don't want my pick. I want what I had – a world I understood, not one I can control.'

'But why?' I asked, at a loss. The wind shifted, and the scent of iron, mixed with tobacco, talcum powder, and cotton, invaded my nostrils.

'Feeding time already?' Damon asked wryly. 'Haven't you done enough damage?'

'Who cares about one whore in a filthy brothel!' I yelled in frustration. I gestured out to the sea. 'The world is filled with humans, and as soon as one dies, another appears. What does it matter if I relieve one wretched soul of its misery?'

'You're being careless, you know,' Damon grunted. His tongue darted out of his mouth to lick his dry, cracked lips. 'To feed whenever you feel like it. Katherine never did that.'

'Yes, well, Katherine died, didn't she?' I said, my voice much harsher than I meant it to be.

'She'd have hated who you've become,' Damon said, sliding off the fence and standing next to me.

The scent of iron was more pervasive now, curling around me like an embrace.

'No, she would have hated *you*,' I retorted. 'So scared of who you are, unable to go after what you want, wasting your Power.'

I expected Damon to argue, to strike me even. But instead he shook his head, the tips of his retracted canines just visible between his partially open lips.

'I hate myself. I wouldn't expect any different from her,' he said simply.

I shook my head in disappointment. 'What happened to you? You used to be so full of life, so ready for adventure. This is the best thing that has ever happened to us. It's a gift – one that *Katherine* gave to you.'

Across the street, an old man hobbled past, and then

a moment later, a child on an errand rushed by in the opposite direction.

'Pick one and feed! Pick something, anything. Anything is better than just sitting here, letting the world go by.'

With that I stood, following the iron and tobacco scent, feeling my fangs pulse with the promise of a new meal. I grabbed Damon, who lagged a few paces behind me, until we found ourselves on a slanted lane out of range of the gaslights. What little light there was gathered onto a single point: a white-uniformed nurse, leaning against a brick building, smoking a cigarette.

The woman looked up, her startled expression turning into a slow smile as she took in Damon. Typical. Even as a blood-starved vampire, Damon, with his shock of dark hair, long lashes, and broad shoulders, caused women to look twice.

'Want a smoke?' she asked, blowing smoke into concentric circles that blended with the mist in the air.

'No,' Damon said hastily. 'Come on, brother.'

I ignored him, stepping towards her. Her uniform was spattered with blood. I couldn't stop staring at it and the way the rich red contrasted to the stark white. No matter how often I had seen it since changing, blood continued to awe me with its beauty.

'Having a bad night?' I asked, leaning next to her against the building.

Damon grabbed my arm and started to pull me towards the lights of the hospital. 'Brother, let's go.'

Tension coiled in my body. 'No!' It took a swat of my arm to toss him against the wall.

The nurse dropped her cigarette. The ash sparked, then extinguished. I felt the bulge of my fangs behind my lips. It was just a matter of time now.

Damon struggled to his feet, crouching low as if I was going to strike him again.

'I won't watch this,' he said. 'If you do this, I will never forgive you.'

'I have to get back to my shift,' the nurse muttered, taking a step away from me, as if to run.

I grabbed her arm and pulled her to me. She let out one short yelp before I covered her mouth with my hand. 'No need to worry about that anymore,' I hissed, sinking my teeth into her neck.

The liquid tasted like rotting leaves and antiseptic, as if the death and decay of the hospital had invaded her body. I spat the still warm liquid into the gutter and threw the nurse to the ground. Her face was twisted in a grimace of fear.

Stupid girl. She should have sensed the danger and run while she still could. It hadn't even been a hunt. Worthless. She groaned, and I wrapped my fingers against her throat and squeezed until I heard the satisfying crack of bone breaking. Her head hung at an unnatural angle, blood still dripping from the wound.

She wasn't making any noise now.

I turned towards Damon, who stared at me, a horrified expression on his face.

'Vampires kill. It's what we do, brother,' I said calmly, my gaze locking on Damon's blue eyes.

'It's what *you* do,' he said, taking off the coat around his shoulders and throwing it over the nurse. 'Not me. Never me.'

Anger pulsed like a heart at the very core of my being. 'You're weak,' I growled.

'Maybe so,' Damon said. 'But I'd rather be weak than a monster.' His voice grew strong. 'I want no part in your killing spree. And if our paths ever cross again, I swear I will avenge all of your murders, brother.'

Then he spun on his heel and ran at vampire speed down the alleyway, instantly disappearing into the swirling mist.

CHAPTER 8

October 4, 1864

As a human, I'd thought it was my mother's death that had shaped the men Damon and I would become. I'd called myself a half-orphan in the initial days after she died, locking myself away in my room, feeling as though my life had ended at the young age of ten. Father believed grieving was weak and unmanly, so Damon had been the one to comfort me. He'd go riding with me, let me join the older boys in their games, and beat up the Giffin brothers when they made fun of me for crying about Mother during a baseball game. Damon had always been the strong one, my protector.

But I was wrong. It is my own death that has shaped me.

Now the tables have turned. I am the strong one, and I

have been trying to be Damon's protector. But while I have always been grateful to Damon, he despises me and blames me for what he has become. I had forced him to feed from Alice, a bartender at the local tavern, which had completed his transformation. But does that make me a villain? I think not, especially as the act had saved his life.

Finally, I see Damon the way Father had seen him: too imperious, too wilful, too quick to make up his mind, and too slow to change it.

And as I had also realized earlier this evening as I stood just outside the dim glare of the gas lamp, the body of the dead nurse at my feet: I am alone. A full orphan. Just as Katherine had presented herself when she came to Mystic Falls and stayed in our guest house.

So that's how vampires do it, then. They exploit vulnerability, get humans to trust them, and then, when all the emotions are firmly in place, they attack.

So that is what I will do. I know not how or who my next victim will be, but I know, more than ever, that the only person I can look out for and protect is myself. Damon is on his own, and so am I.

I heard Damon steal through the city, moving at vampire speed down the streets and alleys. At one point, he paused, whispering Katherine's name over and over again, like a mantra or a prayer. Then, nothing . . .

Was he dead? Had he drowned himself? Or was he simply too far away for me to hear him?

Either way, the result was the same. I was alone – I'd lost my only connection to the man I'd once been: Stefan Salvatore, the dutiful son, the lover of poetry, the man who stood up for what was right.

I wondered if that meant that Stefan Salvatore, with no one to remember him, was really, truly dead, leaving me to be . . . anyone.

I could move to a different city every year, see the whole world. I could assume as many identities as I'd like. I could be a Union soldier. I could be an Italian businessman.

I could even be Damon.

The sun plunged past the horizon like a cannonball falling to earth, dipping the city into darkness. I turned from one gas-lit street to the next, the soles of my boots rasping over the gravelly cobblestones. A loose newspaper blew towards me. I stomped on the broadsheet, examining an etched photo of a girl with long, dark hair and pale eyes.

She looked vaguely familiar. I wondered if she was a relative of one of the Mystic Falls girls. Or perhaps a nameless cousin who'd attended barbecues at Veritas. But then I saw the headline: BRUTAL MURDER ABOARD THE ATLANTIC EXPRESS.

Lavinia. Of course.

I'd already forgotten her. I reached down and crumpled the paper, hurling it as far as I could into the Mississippi. The surface of the water was muddy and turbulent, dappled with moonlight. I couldn't see my reflection – couldn't see anything but an abyss of blackness as deep and dark as my new future. Could I go for eternity, feeding, killing, forgetting, then repeating the cycle?

Yes. Every instinct and impulse I had screamed yes.

The triumph of closing in on my prey, touching my canines to the paper-thin skin that covered their necks, hearing their hearts slow to a dull thud and feeling a body go limp in my arms . . . Hunting and feeding made me feel alive, whole; they gave me a purpose in the world.

It was, after all, the natural order of things. Animals killed weaker animals. Humans killed animals. I killed humans. Every species had their foe. I shuddered to think what monster was powerful enough to hunt me.

The salty breeze wafting from the water was laced with the odour of unwashed bodies and rotting food – a far cry from the aroma across town, where scents of floral perfume and talcum powder hung heavy in the air of the wide streets. Here shadows hugged every corner, whispers rose and fell with the flowing of the river, and drunken hiccups pierced the air. It was dark, here. Dangerous.

I quite liked it.

I turned a corner, following my nose like a bloodhound on the trail of a doe. I flexed my arms, ready for a hunt – a gin-soaked drunk, a soldier, a lady out after dark. The victim didn't matter.

I turned again, and the iron-scent of blood came closer. The smell was sweet and smoky. I focused on it, on the anticipation of sinking my fangs into a neck, of wondering whose blood I'd be drinking, whose life I'd be stealing.

I continued to walk, picking up my pace as I traced the scent to an anonymous back street lined with an apothecary, a general store, and a tailor. The street was a replica of our own Main Street back in Mystic Falls. But while we'd only had one, New Orleans must have had dozens, if not hundreds, of these corridors of commerce.

The rusty smell of iron was stronger now. I followed twists and turns, my hunger building, burning, searing my very skin until finally, finally I came to a squat, peach-coloured building. But when I saw the painted sign above the door, I stopped short. Sausages in their casings hung in the building's grimy window; slabs of cured meat dangled from the ceiling like a grotesque child's mobile; carved ribs were nestled in ice beneath a counter, and in the far back, whole carcasses were strung up, draining blood into large vats.

This was a . . . butcher shop?

I sighed in frustration but my hunger forced me to push the door open anyway. The iron chain snapped easily, as if it were no sturdier than thread. Once inside, I gazed at the bloodied carcasses, momentarily mesmerized by the blood falling into the vats, one drip at a time.

Over the sound of the raining blood, I heard the slightest *ping*, no louder than the twitch of a mouse's whiskers. Then came the light shuffle of toes passing over concrete.

I reared back, my eyes darting from corner to corner. Mice scuttled beneath the floorboards, and someone's watch ticked in the building next door. All else was quiet. But the air around me suddenly felt thicker, and the ceiling lower somehow, and I became acutely aware that there was no back exit in this room of death.

'Who goes there?' I called into the darkness, whirling around, my fangs bared. And then came movement. Fangs, eyes, the thud of footsteps closed in around me from all corners.

A low, guttural growl echoed off the bloodstained walls of the shop, and I realized with a sickening jolt that I was surrounded by vampires who looked all too ready to pounce.

CHAPTER 9

I crouched low, my fangs elongated. The heady scent of blood permeated every corner of the room, making my head spin. It was impossible to know where to attack first.

The vampires growled again, and I emitted a low snarl in response. The circle closed in tighter around me. There were three of them, and I was caught, like a fish in a net, a deer surrounded by wolves.

'What do you think you're doing?' one of the vampires asked. He looked to be in his mid-twenties and had a scar that ran the length of his face, from his left eye to the corner of his lip.

'I'm one of you,' I said, standing at my full height, fangs on display.

'Oh, he's one of us!' an older vampire said in a singsongy voice. He wore glasses and a tweed vest over a white-collared shirt. But for the fangs and red-rimmed eyes, he could have been an accountant or a friend of my father's.

I kept my face impassive. 'I have no ill business with you, brothers.'

'We are not your brothers,' said another with tawny hair. He looked not a day over fifteen. His face was smooth, but his green eyes were hard.

The older one stepped forward, poking his bony finger against my chest as if it were a wooden stake. 'So, brother, nice evening to dine . . . or die. What do you think?'

The young vampire kneeled next to me, gazing into my eyes. 'Looks like he'll do both tonight. Lucky boy,' he said, ruffling my hair. I tried to kick him, but my foot simply flopped harmlessly against air.

'No, no, no.' While the scarred vampire watched wordlessly, the boy grabbed my arms and wrenched them so sharply and abruptly behind my back that I gasped. 'Don't be disrespectful. We're your elders. And you've already done quite enough disrespecting already, if Miss Molly's house is any indication.' He drawled her name as if he were a benign, genteel Southern gentleman. Only the steel grip on my limbs betrayed that he wasn't anything of the sort.

'I didn't do anything,' I said, kicking again. If I were to die, then I'd die in a fight.

'Are you sure?' he asked, looking down at me in disgust. I attempted to twist away, but still I couldn't budge.

The elder vampire chuckled. 'Can't control his urges. Impulsive, this one. Let's give him a taste of his own medicine.' With a flourish, he released me from his grasp, pushing me forward with strength I'd never before felt. I hit the plaster wall with a crash and fell on my shoulder, my head cracking against the wooden floorboards.

I cowered beneath my attackers, the realization sinking in that if I were to survive this encounter, it would not be by might. 'I didn't mean to do anything. I'm sorry,' I said, my voice breaking on the word.

'Do you mean it?' the young vampire asked, a glint in his eye. The sound of wood breaking assaulted my ears. I flinched. Would one vampire stake another? This was not a question I wanted answered the hard way.

'Yes. Yes! I didn't mean to come in here. I didn't know anyone was here. I only just arrived in New Orleans,' I said, scrambling for an excuse.

'Silence!' he commanded, advancing towards me, a jagged piece of wood in his hand. I pressed my spine into the damaged wall. So this is how it would end. With me dying on a makeshift stake, killed by my own kind.

Two hands crushed my arms, while another two pinned my ankles together so forcefully that it felt as though I were stuck under boulders. I closed my eyes. An image of Father lying prone on his study floor swam to the forefront of my mind, and I shook my head in agony, remembering his sweating, terrified face. Of course, I'd been trying to save him, but he hadn't known that. If he was watching, as an angel or a demon or a mere spectre condemned to haunt the world, he'd be thrilled to see this scene unfold.

I squeezed my eyes tighter, trying to evoke some other memory to the fore of my mind, one that would take me to another place, another time. But all I could think of were my victims, of the moment when my fangs sliced into their skin, their plaintive wails descending into silence, the blood dripping down my fangs and onto my chin. Soon, all the blood I'd taken would be released, seeping out of my own body and back into the earth, as I was left to die, for real this time, forever, on this wooden floor.

'Enough!' A female voice sliced through the montage in my mind. Immediately, the vampires let go of my hands and feet. My eyes sprang open, and I saw a woman gliding through a narrow wooden door in the back. Her long blonde hair descended in a single plait down her back, and she wore men's black breeches and braces. She was tall, though slight as a child, and all the other vampires shrank away from her in fear.

'You,' she said, kneeling next to me. 'Who are you?' Her amber eyes gazed into mine. They were clear and curious, but there was something about them – the darkness of the pupils, perhaps – that seemed ancient and knowing, which stood in sharp contrast to her rosy-cheeked, unlined face.

'Stefan Salvatore,' I answered her.

'Stefan Salvatore,' she repeated in a perfect Italian accent. Although teasing, her voice didn't seem unkind. She ran a finger gently along my jaw, then placed her palm against my chest and pressed me against the wall, hard. The suddenness of the movement stunned me, but as I sat, pinned and helpless, she brought her other wrist to her mouth, using her fang to puncture the vein. She dragged her wrist along her teeth, creating a small stream of blood.

'Drink,' she commanded, bringing her wrist to my lips.

I did as I was told, managing to get a few drops of the liquid down my throat before she yanked her hand away. 'That's enough. That should fix your wounds at any rate.'

'He and his brother have been wreaking havoc all over town,' the large vampire said, his makeshift stake pointed at me like a rifle.

'Just me,' I said quickly. 'My brother had no part in it.' Damon would never survive the wrath of these demons. Not in his weakened state.

The blonde vampire wrinkled her nose as she leaned even closer towards me.

'You're what, a week old?' she asked, leaning back on her heels.

'Almost two weeks,' I said defiantly, lifting my chin.

She nodded, a hint of a smile on her lips, and stood, surveying the shop. The plaster wall was partially caved in, and blood smeared the floor and speckled the walls, as though a child had stood in the centre of the room and twirled around with a wet paintbrush. She tsked, and the three male vampires simultaneously took a step back. I shivered.

'Percy, come here, and bring that knife,' she said.

With a sigh, the youngest vampire produced a long carving knife from behind his back.

'He wasn't following the rules,' he said petulantly, reminding me of the Giffin boys back home. They were both bullies, always ready to kick a kid in the schoolyard and then turn around and tell a teacher they had nothing to do with it.

She took the knife and stared at it, running the pad of her index finger over the gleaming blade. Then she held it back out to Percy. He hesitated a moment, but finally stepped forward to take it. Just then the girl's canines elongated and her eyes flushed blood-red. With a growl, she stabbed Percy right in the chest. He fell to his knees, doubled over in silent agony.

'You hunt this vampire for making a scene in town,' she seethed, stabbing the knife in farther, 'and yet you attempt to destroy him in this public space, in this shop? You're just as foolish as he is.'

The young vampire staggered to his feet. Blood streamed down the front of his shirt, as though he'd spilled coffee on himself. He grimaced as he pulled the knife out with a sucking sound. 'I'm sorry,' he gasped.

'Thank you.' The woman held her wrist towards Percy's mouth. Despite her youthful look and apparently violent temper, she also had a mothering quality that the other vampires seemed to accept, as if her stabbings were as normal to them as a light swat would be to a high-spirited child.

She turned towards me. 'I'm sorry for your troubles, Stefan. Now, can I help you be on your way?' she asked.

I looked around wildly. I'd thought no further ahead than escaping this room. 'I . . .'

'. . . don't have anywhere to go,' she said with a sigh, finishing my thought. She glanced towards the other vampires, who were now huddled in the corner of the room, heads bent in conversation.

'I'll just be going,' I said, struggling to my feet. My leg was fine, but my arms shook, and my breath came erratically. With local vampires watching my every move, where would I go? How would I feed?

'Nonsense, you're coming with us,' she said, turning on

her heel and walking out the door. She pointed to the young vampire and the one who wore glasses. 'Percy and Hugo, stay and clean this place up.'

I had to practically run to keep up with her and the tall, scarred vampire who'd watched my torture. 'You'll need someone to show you around,' she explained, pausing only slightly. 'This is Buxton,' she said, grabbing the elbow of the vampire with the long scar.

We walked down street after street until we neared a church with a tall spire.

'We're here,' she said, turning sharply to enter a wrought-iron gate. Her boots echoed against a slate path that led to the rear of a house. She opened the door, and a musty scent greeted me. Buxton immediately walked through the parlour and up a set of stairs, leaving me and the young female vampire alone in the darkness.

'Welcome home,' she said, spreading her hands wide. 'There are plenty of spare rooms upstairs. Find one that suits you.'

'Thank you.' As my eyes adjusted to the darkness, I took in my surroundings. Black velvet curtains fastened with golden rope blocked every window. Dust motes floated in the air, and gilt-framed paintings covered the walls. The furniture was threadbare, and I could just make out two sweeping staircases with what looked like oriental runners and, in the next room, a piano. Though at one point this must have been a grand house, now the soiled walls were cracked and peeling, and cobwebs draped over the gold-and-crystal chandelier above us.

'Always enter through the back. Never draw back the curtains. Don't ever bring anyone here. Do you understand, Stefan?' She looked at me pointedly.

'Yes,' I said, running a finger along the marble fireplace, cutting a path in the inch-thick dust.

'Then I think you will like it here,' she said.

I turned to face her, nodding in agreement. My panic had subsided, and my arms no longer trembled.

'I'm Lexi,' she said, holding out her hand, allowing me to raise it to my lips and kiss it. 'I have a feeling that you and I will be friends for a long time.'

CHAPTER 10

I awoke next as dusk was settling over the city. From my window, I could see the goldfish-orange sun sinking low behind a white steeple. The entire house was silent, and for a moment, I couldn't remember where I was. Then everything came back: the butcher shop, the vampires, me being flung against the wall.

Lexi.

As if on cue, she glided into the room, barely making a sound as she pushed open the door. Her blonde hair was loose around her shoulders, and she was wearing a simple black dress. If looked at quickly, she could be mistaken for a child. But I could tell from the slight creases around her eyes and the fullness of her lips that she'd been a full-grown woman, probably around nineteen or twenty. I had no idea how many years she'd seen since then.

She perched on the edge of my bed, smoothing back my hair.

'Good evening, Stefan,' she said, a mischievous glint in her eye. She clutched a tumbler of dark liquid between her fingers. 'You slept,' she noted.

I nodded. Until I'd sunk into the feather bed on the third floor of the house, I hadn't realized that I'd barely slept in the past week. Even on the train, I'd always been twitching, aware of the sighs and snores of my fellow passengers and always, *always* the steady thrum of blood coursing through their veins. But here no heartbeats had kept me from slumber.

'I brought this for you,' she said, proffering the glass. I pushed it away. The blood in it smelled stale, sour.

'You need to drink,' she said, sounding so much like me speaking to Damon that I couldn't help but feel a tiny pang of irritation – and sorrow. I brought the tumbler to my lips and took a tiny sip, fighting the urge to spit it out. As I expected, the drink tasted like dank water and the scent made me feel vaguely ill.

Lexi smiled to herself, as if enjoying a private joke. 'It's goat's blood. It's good for you. You'll make yourself sick, the way you were feeding. A diet made exclusively of human blood isn't good for the digestion. Or the soul.'

'We don't have souls,' I scoffed. But I brought the cup to my lips once more.

Lexi sighed and took the tumbler, placing it on the nightstand next to me. 'So much to learn,' she whispered, almost to herself.

'Well, we have nothing but time, right?' I pointed out. I was rewarded with a rich laugh, which was surprisingly loud and throaty coming from her waif-like body.

'You catch on quickly. Come. Get up. It's time to show you our city,' she said, handing me a plain white shirt and trousers.

After changing, I followed her down the creaking wooden stairs to where the other vampires milled about in the ballroom. They were dressed up, but all looked faintly old-fashioned, as if they'd stepped out of one of the many portraits on the wall. Hugo sat at the piano, playing an out-of-tune rendition of Mozart while wearing a blue velvet cape. Buxton, the hulking, violent vampire, was wearing a loose, ruffled, white shirt, and Percy had on faded breeches and braces that made him look as though he were running late to play a game of ball with his schoolmates.

When they saw me, the vampires froze. Hugo managed a slight nod, but the rest merely stared in stony silence.

'Let's go!' Lexi commanded, leading our group out the door, down the slate path, through zigzagging alleyways, and finally onto a street marked Bourbon. Each entryway led to a dimly lit bar, from which inebriated patrons stumbled out into the night air. Suggestively clad women gathered in clumps beneath awnings, and revellers acted punch-drunk, ready to laugh or fight at a moment's notice. I instantly knew why Lexi took us here. Despite our odd attire, we attracted no more attention than any of the other lively revellers.

As we walked, the others flanked me, keeping me in the centre of their circle at all times. I knew I was being watched sharply, and I tried to remain unaffected by the scent of blood and the rhythm of beating hearts.

'Here!' Lexi said, not bothering to consult the rest of the group as she pushed open a saloon door that read MILADIES in curlicue script. I was impressed by her boldness – back in Mystic Falls, only women of ill repute would ever enter a bar-room. But as I was fast realizing, New Orleans wasn't Mystic Falls.

The floor of Miladies was caked with sawdust, and I winced at the overwhelmingly acrid smell of sweat, whiskey, and cologne. The tables were packed shoulder to shoulder with men playing cards, gambling, and gossiping. One entire side of the room was filled with Union soldiers, and in another corner, a motley band consisting of players with an accordion, two fiddles, and a flute was playing a jaunty rendition of 'The Battle Hymn of the Republic'.

'What do you think?' Lexi asked, leading me to the bar.

'Is this a Union bar?' I asked. The Union army had

captured the city some months back, and soldiers stood sentinel on nearly every corner, maintaining order and reminding Confederates that the war they were fighting looked to be a losing cause.

'Yes. You know what that means, right?'

I scanned the room. Aside from the soldiers, it was a solitary crowd. Single men drowned their loneliness at wooden tables, barely acknowledging their neighbours. The bartenders filled glasses with a mechanical air, never seeming to register the people for whom they poured their wares.

I understood immediately. 'Everyone here is a stranger passing through.'

'Exactly.' Lexi smiled, clearly pleased that I was catching on.

Buxton cleared his throat in disapproval. I could tell he didn't like me – that he was waiting for me to slip up so he could stake me without incurring Lexi's wrath.

'Hugo, find us a table!' Lexi commanded. Hugo walked his hulkish frame over to a rough-hewn table next to the band. Before he could even open his mouth, the blue-coated soldiers at the table glanced at each other and stood up, leaving half-filled mugs behind.

Lexi pulled out two chairs. 'Stefan, sit next to me.'

I sat, vaguely embarrassed that I was so compliant, like a child. But I reminded myself that even Hugo followed her lead. Lexi had Power, and she knew how to use it.

Percy, Hugo and Buxton also settled around.

'Now,' Lexi said, taking one of the abandoned beer mugs and waving it around in the air, just as the waitress approached us. 'Let's teach you how to behave in public.'

My cheeks flushed with anger. 'I am behaving,' I said through clenched teeth. 'Despite the fact that there are so many people that it's nearly impossible to concentrate.'

Percy and Hugo snickered.

'He's not ready . . .' Buxton said in a surly tone.

'Yes, he is.' Lexi's words were low and slightly menacing. Buxton clenched his jaw, clearly trying to rein in his temper. I shifted in my chair. I suddenly felt like I was ten years old again, with Damon protecting me from the Giffin brothers. Only this time it was a girl standing up for me. I was about to point out that I didn't need Lexi to answer for me when she placed a hand on my knee. The touch was gentle and calmed me.

'It gets easier,' she said, briefly catching my eyes. 'So, lesson one,' she stated, addressing the entire group. A kindness on her part, I realized, since I was the only one who didn't know the finer points of being a vampire. 'Lesson one is learning how to compel without drawing attention to yourself.' She leaned back and eyed the band. 'I don't like this song. Stefan, what song would you like to hear?'

'Uh . . .' I glanced around the table, confused. Percy snickered again, but stopped when Lexi glared at him. '"God Save the South"?' I said hesitantly. The first thing that came to my head, it was a tune Damon used to whistle when he was on leave from the army.

Lexi scooted her chair back, the legs kicking up a layer of sawdust. She sauntered over to the band and looked each of the members in the eye as she said something I couldn't hear.

The band stopped mid-chord and immediately switched to 'God Save the South'.

'Hey!' one soldier shouted. His comrades glanced at one another, clearly wondering why a band in a Union bar had suddenly been inspired to play a pro-Southern song.

Lexi grinned, as if delighted by her trick. 'Are you impressed?'

'Very,' I said, meaning it. Even Percy and Hugo nodded in agreement.

Lexi took a sip of her beer. 'Your turn. Pick someone,' she said.

I glanced around the bar, my eye catching on a dark-haired barmaid. Her eyes were deep brown, and her hair was tied in a low knot at the nape of her neck. Her lips were parted, and she wore a cameo pendant that nestled in the dip of her neck. In the split second between seeing and knowing, I was reminded of Katherine. I thought of my first glimpse of Miss Molly, and how I'd mistaken her for Katherine as well. It felt as though my maker were intent to haunt me in New Orleans.

'Her,' I said, nodding towards the girl.

Lexi looked at me sharply, as if she knew there was a story behind this decision. But she didn't pry. 'Clear your mind,' she said instead, 'and allow your energy to enter her.'

I nodded, remembering the moment on the train when my thoughts had touched Lavinia's. I fixed my gaze on the barmaid. She was laughing, her head tilted back towards the ceiling, but as soon as my focus locked on her, her eyes lowered to mine, almost as if I'd bidden her to do so.

'Good,' Lexi murmured. 'Now, use your mind to tell her what you want from her.'

That was the piece I had missed. When I'd tried to compel the conductor, I'd had thousands of thoughts about possible scenarios that could happen during our interaction, but I had not asked for any of them.

Come here, I willed, staring into her liquid chocolate eyes. *Come to me*. For a moment she held her place behind the bar, but then she took a hesitant step forward. *Yes, keep going*. She stepped forward again, more confidently this time, making her way towards me. I had expected her to look dazed, almost as though she were sleepwalking. But she didn't appear to be in a trance. To any bystander, she could have simply been coming to our table to take our drink orders.

'Hello,' I said when she reached us.

'Don't break eye contact,' Lexi whispered. 'Tell her what you want her to do now.'

Sit down, I thought. And, almost instantly, the girl wedged herself between me and Buxton, her thigh warm against mine.

'Hello,' she said unblinkingly. 'It's the strangest thing, but suddenly I just knew that I needed to sit here with you.'

'I'm Stefan,' I said, shaking her hand. My fangs elongated, and the sides of my stomach knocked together. I wanted her. Badly.

'Don't embarrass us,' came Lexi's final words before she turned from me to face the band. It was clear that while she wasn't condoning any of my subsequent actions, she wasn't necessarily condemning them.

Invite me outside, I thought, placing my hand on the barmaid's thigh. But even as I thought the words, I glanced at Lexi, breaking my connection with the girl.

The girl shifted, pulled her hair up, then dropped it down on her back. She glanced at the band, rubbing her forefinger on the rim of a glass.

Invite me outside, I thought again, refocusing my attention fully on her. Sweat prickled my temple. Had I lost the connection for good?

But then she gave a slight nod. 'You know, it's awfully loud in here, and I want to speak with you. Would you mind if we went outside?' she asked, staring at me.

I stood up, my chair scraping against the floor. 'I'd like that very much,' I said, offering her my arm.

'Bring her back alive, boy, or you'll be answering to me,' said a voice so low that I wondered if I'd imagined it.

But when I turned back, Lexi merely smiled and waved.

CHAPTER 11

Outside, I let the girl lead me away from the drunken crowd and towards a side alley beyond a bar called Calhoun's.

'I'm sorry,' she said breathlessly. 'I don't know what came over me. I'm usually not so fresh, it's just that—'

'I'm thankful for it,' I said, interrupting her. She shivered, and I put my arms around her thin frame. Instantly, she pulled away.

'You're so cold!' she said in an accusatory tone.

'Am I?' I asked, feigning nonchalance. *You want to kiss me*, I thought.

She shrugged. 'It's OK. It's just that I'm sensitive to temperature. But I know a way we could both warm up.' She smiled shyly, then raised up to her tiptoes. Her lips pressed against mine, and for a moment, I allowed myself to enjoy their warmth and feel the girl's blood race through her veins as she gave herself over to me.

Then I lunged for her neck.

'Ow!' She protested, trying to push me off. 'Stop!'

You will succumb, because if you do that, I'll let you live, I thought, using every fibre of my being to compel her at this crucial moment. She gazed up at me, confusion in her eyes, before she fell back over my arms, her face a mask of sleepy satisfaction.

I took a few more sips of the blood, all too conscious of Lexi and the others back inside. Then I dragged the woman up to her feet. I'd been careful. The holes I'd made in her neck were tiny, almost impossible to see with human vision. Still, I adjusted her scarf around her neck to cover them up.

'Wake up,' I whispered softly.

Her eyes opened, the gaze unfocused. 'What . . . where am I?' I could sense her heart beating faster, sense her ready to let loose a scream.

'You were helping a drunk customer,' I told her. 'You are free to go. I was simply making sure you were OK.'

She snapped to attention, her body relaxing. 'I apologize, sir. Usually, the patrons don't get so rowdy at Miladies. Thank you for assisting me. I'll give you a whiskey, on the house,' she said, winking at me.

I walked into Miladies beside her, and was rewarded with Lexi's slow smile from the corner table.

Good job, boy.

I followed the girl until she safely resumed her position behind the polished wood counter of the bar.

'What's your poison?' she asked, whiskey bottle in hand. She looked pale, as if she were coming down with a slight cold. Meanwhile, her blood was warm in my stomach.

'I've drunk quite enough, thank you, miss,' I said, as I took her hand and brought it up to my lips, kissing it as tenderly as I'd marked her neck.

CHAPTER 12

The following evening Lexi knocked on my bedroom door. She wore a black coat and matching trousers. A cap hid most of her hair, save for a few blonde tendrils that fell loose and framed her face.

'I was proud of you last night,' she said. I smiled, despite myself. It was surprising how quickly I took to seeking Lexi's approval. 'How much did you take from the barmaid?'

'Not too much. But I wanted more,' I admitted.

A look I couldn't quite decipher passed over her face. 'I used to be like you, you know. But the more you feed from humans, the hungrier you get. It's a curse. But there are other ways. Have you hunted for animals' blood?'

I shook my head no.

'Well, luckily for you, I'm going hunting now,' she said, 'and you're coming with me. Put on dark clothes and meet me downstairs in five minutes.'

I shrugged on a dark, military-looking jacket I'd found hanging in the closet and raced downstairs, loath to put off hunting with Lexi for even five minutes. While I bristled at Buxton's comments about how inexperienced I was, when I heard it from Lexi, I was only eager for a lesson on how our kind survived.

We walked out the door, no trace of sunlight in the inky black sky. I sniffed the air, searching out the scent of the nearest human, then stopped when I saw Lexi staring at me with a knowing look.

Instead of turning left, towards the bustle of Bourbon Street, she turned right, snaking through side streets until we reached a forest. Above us the trees were bare and ghostly against the dark night sky, the moon our only light.

'There are deer here,' Lexi said, 'and squirrels, bears, rabbits. I think there's a den of foxes that way,' she added, walking into the thick, mossy woods. 'Their blood smells earthier than human blood, and their hearts beat much more rapidly.'

I followed her lead. Quickly and silently, we darted from tree to bush without disturbing the underbrush. In a way, it felt like we were playing a game of hide-and-seek, or just playing at hunting, the way young schoolboys do. After all, as a human, I'd always carried a weapon on the hunt. Now all I had were my fangs.

Lexi held up a hand. I paused, midstep, my eyes darting everywhere. I didn't see anything but thick trunks and racing ants in jagged stumps. Then, without warning, Lexi lunged. When she stood up, blood was dripping from her fangs, and a self-satisfied smile appeared on her face. A creature lay on the fallen leaves, its legs bent as if it were still mid-run.

She gestured to the lump of orangish-red fur. 'Fox isn't bad. Would you like to try it?'

I knelt down, my lips curling as they made contact with the rough fur. I forced myself to gingerly take a sip of liquid, though, as I knew it was what Lexi wanted. I sucked in, and immediately the blood seared my tongue. I spat it out violently.

'Fox is an acquired taste, I suppose,' Lexi said as she knelt on the ground by my side. 'More for me, at least!'

While Lexi fed, I leaned against a tree trunk and listened to the rustling sounds of the forest. The breeze shifted, and suddenly the scent of iron-rich blood was everywhere. It was sweet and spicy, and it wasn't coming from Lexi's fox.

Somewhere, nearby, there was a human heart, beating out seventy-two *thu-thuds* a minute.

Cautiously I slipped past Lexi, and ventured out past the perimeter of the forest. Set up on the edge of the lake was a shanty town. Tents were pitched at every angle, and makeshift clotheslines ran between wooden posts. The whole set-up looked haphazard, as if the inhabitants knew they'd have to pick up and relocate at any second.

The camp looked deserted save for one woman who was bathing, the moonlight striking her ivory skin. She was humming to herself, washing the caked dirt off her hands and face.

I hid behind a large oak tree, intending to take the woman by surprise. But then a large painted poster on a neighbouring tree caught my eye. I took a step towards it. A branch cracked, the woman whirled around, and I could sense Lexi behind me.

'Stefan,' Lexi murmured, obviously aware of the unfolding scene. But this time, I was the one to hold up my hand to silence her. Mist floated over the portrait on the sign, but the printing was clear: PATRICK GALLAGHER'S FREAK SHOW: VAMPIRE VERSUS BEAST. BATTLE TO THE DEATH! OCTOBER 8.

I blinked, and the portrait swam into my vision. It was of a dark-haired man with chiselled features and pale-blue eyes. His teeth were bared, his canines elongated, and he was crouched opposite a snarling mountain lion.

I knew the face on the poster better than I knew my own.

It was Damon.

CHAPTER 13

Damon. Death.

The words swam in my mind as I tried to make sense of what I was seeing. Damon was alive. But who knew for how long? If he had been captured, he was undoubtedly weak. How could he face a ravenous beast in a battle and survive?

Anger tore through my body, along with the familiar ache of my fangs elongating. I ripped down the sign with a snarl.

'What is it?' Lexi hissed, her own fangs bared.

I held up the paper.

'My brother,' I said, staring without comprehension at the poster. The picture made him look like a monster. My eye twitched. 'The battle is in two days.'

Lexi nodded, taking in the portrait.

'Gallagher found him,' she said, almost to herself.

I shook my head, not understanding what she meant.

She sighed. 'Big businessman. He owns a lot of places in

town, including a two-bit circus and freak show. Always looking for curiosities to display, and people always seem to find the money to attend. Your brother—'

'Damon,' I said, cutting her off. 'His name is Damon.'

'Damon,' Lexi said gently, tracing the image with her fingers.

'He doesn't deserve this,' I said, almost to myself. 'I need to help him. But . . .' I trailed off. But what? How could I possibly save him?

'We'll need to find him,' Lexi decided. She brushed leaves and dirt from the back of her trousers. 'Do you trust me?'

Did I have a choice? My hunger forgotten, I followed her through the forest and back to the wide, silent streets of the city.

'Gallagher lives somewhere in the Garden District with all the other nouveaux riches. On Laurel Street, I think,' Lexi murmured as we wove our way to the centre of town. 'This has happened before, soon after Gallagher arrived in New Orleans five years ago.'

'What happened?' I asked, following closely behind her in the shadows.

'He found a vampire. He's good at finding us. Or maybe we're good at finding him. But the other vampire wasn't part of my family. And . . .' She stopped suddenly.

'What happened to him?'

But Lexi merely shook her head. We'd arrived at the Garden District, where the streets were wide and the lawns hugging the sherbet-coloured Victorian houses were lush and expansive.

'Here.' She stopped at a pistachio-hued mansion enclosed by an open wrought-iron fence. Magnolias and calla lilies spilled over the gate, and the air smelled like mint. Just beyond, I could see an enormous herb garden that took up a fifth of the property. I recoiled as we walked closer, as the garden grew a generous amount of vervain.

Lexi wrinkled her nose. 'He knows all the tricks,' she said wryly.

We pushed open the gate, our footsteps barely crunching the gravel on the path that circled the house. Cicadas buzzed in the sycamore trees above us, and I could hear horses pacing in the stable.

And then I heard a low moan.

'He's out back,' I said.

Lexi gazed up at the sky. Orange streaks were starting to peek above the horizon; it was about an hour until day broke. 'It's too close to dawn,' Lexi said. 'I didn't realize how late it is. I have to go.'

I looked at her sharply.

'I'm not protected.' Her fingers fluttered to my ring, and I glanced down self-consciously. The lapus lazuli adornment had become so much a part of me, I'd forgotten that it made me different from other vampires, made me able to walk in the daylight. Katherine had arranged for both Damon and me to have this protection.

'We'll come back tomorrow. The others can help us then,' Lexi insisted.

I shook my head. 'I can't leave him.'

Birds chirped in the trees above us, and from somewhere nearby came the sound of glass shattering. The orange streaks in the sky grew fatter, brighter. 'I understand,' Lexi said finally. 'Be safe. Don't play the hero.'

I nodded, scanning the grounds for any guards or animals lying in wait to attack. When I looked up, Lexi was gone and I was alone.

Stealing quickly to the back of the house, I made my way towards the whitewashed stable. Horses pawed the ground nervously, obviously sensing my presence. The stable doors were padlocked with an iron bolt. I grabbed the chain, testing it. Even though I'd barely fed since the previous evening, it would be easy enough to rend the chains with my bare hands. But something stopped me. *Don't play the hero*. Lexi's words echoed in my mind. She had become my guide during the past couple of days, and I knew it was in my best interest to listen to her. Better not to leave any evidence of an intruder, better to get the lie of the land before doing anything rash.

I released the chain, and it fell back against the door with a loud clanking sound. A horse whinnied. I walked to the other side of the stable, where a dusty window was open a crack.

'Brother?' I whispered hoarsely through the window. The cloying scent of vervain was everywhere, making me woozy and nauseated.

In the corner, a filthy figure struggled to sit up. Damon. His hands and feet were bound with chains, and his skin was covered in angry red welts. The chains must have been soaked in vervain. I winced in sympathy.

Damon's eyes locked on mine.

'You found me,' he said, no emotion in his face. 'Are you happy to see that I'm close to death, brother?'

'I'm here to save you,' I said simply. The horses were kicking up the sawdust around their feet in agitation; I didn't have much time before someone in the house heard the disturbance.

Damon shrugged, an effort that clearly took all his energy. His eyes were bloodshot and glassy. A large cut lined his forehead, slicing into his eyebrow. He looked awful and emaciated; it was clear he hadn't eaten in days.

I glanced around, hoping I could find something – a squirrel, a rabbit, a chipmunk – to kill and toss to him, but there was nothing.

'So the cold-blooded killer is going to save me.' Damon attempted a wan smile. He leaned back against the wall, his chains rattling.

'Yes, we have to—'

Suddenly, I heard the sound of a door slamming, then a dog barking. I whirled around towards the main house.

'What do you think you're doing?' a voice yelled out. And I stood, my hands raised to the sky, unsure of who – or what – had found me this time.

CHAPTER 14

My hands still in the air, I pressed my lips together. I'd already learned that any sign of stress caused my fangs to bulge and my pupils to grow larger; I didn't want to prepare to attack until I knew what I was dealing with.

'Jake? Charley?' a female voice called as two burly men ran towards me from the main house. Although twice my bulk, they were definitely human. Each man grabbed one of my arms, though I noted with cold calculation that it would take only one quick twist to shake both off before I lunged for my attack.

But I fought with every core of my being to stay still, my hands high in the air, hoping I'd just look like a common vagrant. There was no guarantee that a fight would lead to Damon's rescue.

A girl walked towards me from the porch and stopped a foot away.

'I apologize,' I said to her. I tried to make my voice sound like I was nervously gasping for breath. 'I didn't realize this was private property. I'm new to town, and I was in the tavern, and, well . . .' I trailed off, unsure of whether my lies would get me into even deeper trouble.

'You thought you'd steal from me?' The girl stepped forward. Her hair tumbled in flaming curls down her back, and she wore what looked suspiciously like a vervain wreath on her head. She had on a white nightdress, but she was wearing men's boots, and I could see calluses on her hands. Though she was clearly from a wealthy family, this was no coddled city girl.

'No. No! I wasn't stealing, I was just looking for the vampire,' I said.

She knitted her eyebrows together. 'To steal him . . . ?' she asked leadingly, hands on her hips.

'No!' I said again, my arm jerking involuntarily. One of the men holding me dropped my arm in surprise. 'No,' I said again, forcing myself to remain still. 'I saw the poster for the show down by the lake, and, well, I guess my curiosity got the better of me.' I shrugged.

A rooster crowed. Sunlight slowly spilled over the backyard. I glanced down at my gleaming ring, thankful that Lexi had left.

'OK, then,' the girl said. She snapped her fingers, and the

two large men dropped my arms. 'If you are new to town, then where do you come from?'

'Mys . . . Mississippi,' I fibbed. 'Right across the river.'

She opened her mouth as if to say something, then closed it. 'Well, welcome to New Orleans,' she said. 'I don't know what things are like back in Mississippi, but you can't go sneaking into people's backyards looking at their livestock. And the next time you may not meet someone as friendly as me.'

I fought my urge to snort at her idea of friendliness, given my brother's wretched state.

'So, what's your name, stranger?'

'Stefan,' I said. 'Are you Miss Gallagher?'

'Smart,' she observed sarcastically. 'That I am. Callie Gallagher.'

One of the large men stepped towards her protectively.

'Leave us,' she commanded. 'I'll escort Mr Stefan out.'

'Thank you,' I said contritely as I followed her around the long gravel path, past the sun-room of the house, and towards the gate. 'Thanks for trusting me,' I said.

'Who says I trust you?' she asked sharply, but an amused smile flitted across her lips.

'Well, then, perhaps I should thank you for not letting your brutes kill me.'

She smiled again, wider this time. Her teeth were pearly

white, and one of her front teeth was slightly crooked. Freckles dusted her upturned nose. She smelled sweet, like oranges. I realized it had been a long time since I had found a woman beautiful for more than the sweet smell of her blood. But cruelty lay behind her beauty, because this woman was responsible for my brother's imprisonment.

'Maybe you're too handsome to be killed. And everyone deserves a little kindness, don't you think?'

I gazed at her calloused hands, a thought entering my mind. 'Would it be too forward of me to ask for more of your kindness?'

Callie narrowed her eyes. 'Depends on what you ask for.'

'A job,' I said, straightening my shoulders.

The girl shook her head incredulously. 'You want me to hire you? After you trespassed on my property?'

'Think of it as an expression of my drive and my enthusiasm for . . . freaks,' I said, the lies now floating easily from my tongue. 'Being new, I've had trouble finding work, and to be honest, I've always wanted to be part of a circus.'

She set her jaw, and I was worried she'd suddenly call her henchmen on me. But then she looked up and down at my faded trousers and sighed. 'I have a feeling I'll regret this, but come down to Lake Road tomorrow night. We do need a new ticket taker – our last one ran off with one of the fat ladies. You'll need to arrive early – and stay late. It's going to be busy tomorrow night because of the fight.'

'Right. The fight,' I said, once again clenching my fists and biting back words of anger.

'Yes.' She smiled somewhat ruefully. 'Then you'll have the chance to see your vampire in action.'

'I suppose I will,' I said, turning on my heel and exiting the wrought-iron gate. But if I had my way, no one would see the 'vampire in action' because Damon and I would be long gone before the fight ever commenced.

CHAPTER 15

October 7, 1864

Something has changed. Maybe it is merely age, a sort of hyper-maturation into the role of an adult vampire. Maybe it is Lexi's tutelage. Or the fact that I am faced with an actual challenge, a death-defying challenge, and I simply know I can't expend my energy killing for sport. Whatever the cause, the result is the same. Though the scent of blood is still everywhere, I no longer feel compelled to hunt for sport. Hunting is distracting. My hunger is something to be sated quickly rather than enjoyably.

Of course, the question is, how will I free Damon? Attack everyone in sight, creating a melee of destruction? Convince Callie to shed her vervain wreath so I can compel her to do my bidding?

But Callie seems to have a power all her own. That

much is clear to her henchmen, and to me.

Of course, my Power is stronger. I have no doubt that I'll persevere. I'll save Damon, and then I'll reward myself with a drink from Callie's neck.

I spent the entire day pacing my room, cutting a path through the dust that lined the wooden floor. Plans to free Damon flitted through my head one by one, but just as quickly as they came, I shot them down for being too daring, too risky, too destructive. I'd already learned from the siege on the vampires in Mystic Falls that one false move can cause a domino effect of violence and despair.

'You look like a caged animal,' Lexi said, appearing at my doorway. Her voice was light, but worry lines creased her forehead.

I let out a low growl and raked my hands through my hair. 'I *feel* like a caged animal.'

'Have you thought of a plan yet?'

'No!' I exhaled loudly. 'And I don't even know why I'm trying. He hates me.' I looked down, suddenly ashamed. 'He blames me for turning him into what we are now.'

Lexi sighed and closed the distance between us. She took my hand. 'Follow me.' She led me out of the room and walked slowly down the stairs, running her pale fingers along the portraits that lined the walls. All the paintings were covered with a layer of grime. I wondered how long they'd been hanging on the walls, and whether any of the subjects still roamed the Earth – alive or undead.

At the very bottom stair, Lexi stopped and pulled a portrait off the wall. It was newer than the others, with a gold frame and the glass polished to a gleam. A young, serious-looking blond boy stared out at me. His blue eyes contained a hint of sadness, and his cleft chin jutted in defiance. He looked incredibly familiar.

My eyes widened. 'Is that your . . .'

'. . . brother,' Lexi said. 'Yes.'

'Is he . . .' I trailed off, not wanting to finish the sentence.

'No, he's not with us anymore,' she said, tracing the cleft of the boy's chin with her index finger.

'How did he die?' I asked.

'Does it matter?' she said, her voice sharp.

'No, I suppose it doesn't.' I touched the edge of the picture. 'Why do you keep it?'

She sighed. 'It's a connection to the past – to who I used to be before I was' – she gestured down the length of her body – 'before I became *this*. It's important not to lose that final thread of attachment to humanity.' Her gaze grew serious.

I knew what she meant: remaining connected to her humanity was how she maintained control and why she made the choice to feed only from animals.

'So, are you ready to save him?'

As usual, Lexi didn't wait for an answer, and I had to hustle out the door behind her. Together, we walked in silence towards Gallagher's place under the cover of the inky night.

Fifteen minutes later we turned the corner onto Laurel Street and the house came into view. A tall man with salt-and-pepper hair was climbing the stairs of the white structure, tapping each step with a gold-tipped cane. Behind him were two black-suited men. The three were engaged in intense conversation.

Lexi put her hand on mine. 'Gallagher.'

The men paused on the porch. 'I'm telling you, the vampire I have is the real thing. I could have him killed and sell you his blood. You'd make a fortune marketing it as the fountain of youth or an elixir of life,' Gallagher said roughly.

My stomach plummeted. Damon's body was being divided before he was even dead.

'Blood,' a stocky man mused, rubbing his bald head as if it were a crystal ball. 'I'm just not sure people would try that. But how much would you sell the fangs for?'

The men entered the home, shutting the wooden door with a definitive thud.

I sniffed the air. The cloying scent of vervain burned my

nose, but I didn't sense Damon anywhere.

Lexi pushed the gates open and stepped onto the lawn.

'What are you doing?' I hissed. 'I don't think Damon's here anymore.'

'Yes, but you need to know exactly who and what you're up against. The more you know, the better you can gauge what the best course of action will be,' she said.

I nodded, and together we stole in the shadows towards the main house. We ducked under a window ledge and knelt in order to escape notice; we could just make out the scene unfolding in the parlour at the back of the house. Gallagher's voice drifted through the open window as he took a seat in a maroon leather club chair, his feet up and a glass of port already in his hands. He wore a large gold ring on his finger.

In the far corner, Callie Gallagher sat in a pair of weathered overalls and a white linen shirt. Her red hair fell down her back in a vervain-laced braid, and her head was bent as she pored over a ledger book. A garland of vervain was strung along the marble mantle, and I noticed a few vampire muzzles – the same sort that my father had used to subdue Katherine – tossed carelessly on an end table.

'I have something else that might interest you,' Gallagher said, locking eyes with the elderly man while the other sat, silently. 'I didn't want to bring it up out on the street.'

'Yes?' The man leaned forward. His voice sounded

disinterested, but he rubbed his stubby fingers together eagerly.

'The monster wears a ring. It's an unusual one. Silver with a blue stone, but it seems to give him additional power. None of my men have been able to get it off his finger, but when he's dead . . .'

'Father!' Callie interjected. The two men stared at her.

'Yes, girl?' Gallagher asked, his voice dangerously low.

'I've been looking over the books, and we'll make a fortune if he's kept alive. It's the best for the show.' Though her expression was all business, her tone didn't actually sound mercenary.

'My boss.' Gallagher laughed ruefully, but from the way the vein in his temple throbbed, I could tell he didn't appreciate Callie's interjection. 'Girl, can you get us some brandy?'

Callie stood up and stalked out of the room. I was surprised to feel a sliver of sympathy – and kinship – with her. I knew what it was like to have a headstrong father. I'd wanted nothing more than to please him, but Giuseppe Salvatore always thought he knew best. I dared to disagree only once, and he killed me for it.

'As I was saying, the ring . . .' Gallagher said. I snapped back to attention.

'You kill that monster and I'll buy it all. The fangs, the

blood, the ring. Everything. And I'll give you a very good price,' the elderly man said in a trembling voice, barely concealing his excitement.

Before I could pounce, shattering the glass that separated me from the man who was trying to sell my brother in bits and pieces, an iron-firm grip clasped my arms behind me and dragged me back out to the street.

'Get a hold of yourself, Stefan!' Lexi hissed as she pulled me along the sidewalk. When she reached the corner of Laurel Street, she let me go.

'That man . . . is a sadist!' I fumed.

'He's a businessman. He wants to kill your brother, and if they find out about you, they'll certainly want to kill you too,' Lexi said, pushing her blonde braid over her shoulder.

My mind spun. 'What about the girl?' I asked.

Lexi snorted derisively. 'What about her?'

'She thinks Damon should be kept alive. Maybe she can convince her father of that,' I said desperately.

'Don't even think about it. She's a human, and she will follow her father's orders until the end of her days,' Lexi said, dropping her voice to lower than a whisper as another couple walked towards us.

As they passed, the man tipped his top hat, and Lexi curtseyed back. To anyone else, we were a young couple, out to romance each other in the moonlight.

'Damon's life is at stake,' I said in frustration. Lexi had offered to help, but everything she'd done so far had seemed designed only to dissuade me. 'We have to do something!'

'I know you will find a way to save him,' she said firmly.

We turned another corner and the spire of the church across from Lexi's house came into view. 'But Stefan, you must remember that controlling yourself around humans is much more than simply not attacking them.' When we reached the back porch, she stopped and put her hands on my shoulders, forcing me to look into her clear amber eyes. 'Do you know the real reason why we don't drink human blood?'

'Why?' I asked.

'Because if we don't drink human blood, we don't need humans,' she said in a tight voice. She pushed open the door. Buxton, Hugo and Percy were sitting around the coffee table, playing poker. They looked up when we entered, and Buxton narrowed his eyes at me.

'Boys, we're going dancing tonight. We need some lightness,' Lexi announced, pouring herself a glass of blood from the decanter on the side table. She glanced around the room. The three nodded. 'Will you come, Stefan?'

I shook my head. I was not in the mood for lightness. 'No,' I said, then headed upstairs to plan Damon's rescue alone.

CHAPTER 16

I searched in vain for peaceful sleep but never found it. Instead when I closed my eyes I saw Damon, his legs curled around a hard wooden chair, his arms bound in ropes. His skin bled, the droplets a dark maroon where the vervain-soaked ropes bit into his flesh.

Next came the images of Callie, her flame-coloured hair flowing behind her, her eyes lit with a frightening passion. She and her father danced around Damon, my brother's form prone on the ground. They threw their hands in the air tauntingly, gripping wooden stakes, the ends so sharpened they reached a fine point. Their movements became more frenzied as they approached, readying their weapons . . .

But worst of all were the visions of Katherine. I would see her, looking beautiful as always, her porcelain face hovering above mine and her glossy mane tickling my shoulders. With a coy, knowing smile she would lean towards me, and then she would open her mouth. Her fangs glinted in the lamp light as they plunged into my neck.

My eyes flew open. Sleep would not afford me any rest. My mind went to memories of Katherine. The human part of me – or what was left of it – hated her with every fibre of my being. My hand curled into a fist involuntarily when I thought of her, and how she'd destroyed my family.

But the vampire part of me missed what she'd represented – stability and love. And just as that part of my soul would last for eternity, so too would the part of me that longed for her. I wanted her now, beside me, curled up in my sheets. I wanted her to lean against the windowsill and listen as I told her about Damon, and tell me, in her calm, even cold, matter-of-fact way what to do. Being with Katherine had made me fearless, confident. She had made everything seem possible.

Even though I trusted Lexi, I knew she didn't trust me to take care of things . . . she didn't believe that any plan I had would work. That was why Lexi reminded me so often of all the obstacles in my path. I longed for the Katherine I had fallen for, the one who seemed both fearless and to truly care for me. I wanted her by my side right now so I would feel less alone. But I knew that couldn't be. That Katherine had never really existed. Besides, she was gone, and she was never coming back.

The door opened, and Lexi stood there, a goblet of animal blood in her hands. She brought it to my lips. I took a few deep sips, despite the disgust it called up in me.

When I had drained the cup, she put it on the nightstand, then brushed my hair off my forehead. 'Are you still going to the fight tonight?'

'Are you going to try to stop me?'

'No.' Lexi bit her lip. 'Not so long as you simply leave it at saving your brother. Revenge is for humans – and killing Gallagher won't teach humans any lesson.'

I nodded, all the while knowing I'd use brute force if it was necessary to free Damon.

'Good.' Lexi turned to leave. Halfway towards the door, she turned back and locked eyes with me, and her expression softened. 'You've cheated death once. I hope you'll cheat it a second time.'

After dressing, I walked to Lake Road with human speed. By the time I got there, it was past dusk. Lanterns and torches were set up around the perimeter of the fairgrounds, making the entire area look as if it was bathed in daylight. The circus tent was striped red and white, and surrounded by midway games and individual booths. 'Fortunes Told!' a poster above one read. 'See the World's Ugliest Woman – If You Dare!' proclaimed another. I could hear the chattering of some type of animal coming from a far corner, but I couldn't get a sense of where Damon was.

Just then, Callie walked out of the main tent, trailed by her father and her two henchmen. She was wearing the same pair of overalls she'd had on the night before over a man's linen shirt, and her hair fell around her shoulders. There was a smudge of dirt beneath her eye. I had a sudden urge to wipe it away but stuck my hands in my pocket instead.

'Stefan!' she called, her face breaking into a smile. 'You're here. Father, this is the man I told you about.'

Mr Gallagher looked even more imposing up close. He towered above me, his dark brows knitted together. I kept my expression open, innocent. Lexi said Gallagher was a skilled vampire hunter – would he be able to detect the truth just by staring at me?

'My daughter says you're curious about vampires,' he said. 'Prove you're serious and work the ticket counter. Then we can talk.'

'Yes, sir.' I nodded, feeling like Stefan the obedient child.

'And, boy?' Gallagher asked, turning back towards me.

'Yes?'

'You want to place a bet on the fight? Winner'll take a lot. Could make you a fortune.' He raised an eyebrow.

My eyes narrowed, and blood screamed through my veins, fast and hot. How dare this man ask me to bet on my brother's life? How dare he act so self-important when I could rip his throat out in an instant?

'Stefan?' Callie asked warily.

Forcing myself to calm down, I reached into the pockets of my well-worn breeches and pulled them inside out. 'I'm afraid I have no money, sir. That's why I'm so grateful to have this job.'

Gallagher took a step closer to me. 'You say you're from Mississippi, boy?' He gazed at me curiously. 'Your accent sounds more northern – maybe Virginian.'

'My parents were from Virginia. I suppose their accent rubbed off on me,' I said in as casual a voice as I could muster.

After a long moment, he nodded. 'Well, when you rustle up some currency, come find me. In the meantime, Callie will show you the ropes. And son?' he called, turning on his heel.

'Yes, sir?' I asked.

'I'll be watching you.'

CHAPTER 17

'Don't be bothered by him,' Callie said, once her father was a safe distance away.

'I'm not,' I lied.

Her green eyes flicked over me, as if she didn't believe my words. But she didn't press the issue.

'I'll give you a quick tour,' she said, taking me into one of the smaller tents. In a corner, a woman was hunched over a mirror. She turned, and I took a step back. Her face was covered with tattoos, which, upon closer inspection, were courtesy of rapidly drying India ink.

'The tattooed woman,' Callie said. 'And the conjoined twins.'

The woman and the twins next to her waved at us. The twins' bodies were connected at the hip. They were beautiful, with blonde hair and sad expressions. A man with flippers instead of arms whispered something in one of their ears. They glanced at each other, then broke into laughter.

'This is the show.' Callie opened her hands wide, and for the first time I noticed a wooden stake dangling on a silver chain from her wrist. She also had a sprig of vervain tucked behind her ear.

'Miss Callie!' A hulking, seven-foot-tall mountain of a man ducked under the door of the tent and walked towards us. He picked her up by her tiny waist and swung her around.

'Arnold!' she said gleefully. 'The world's strongest man. Married to the bearded lady,' she explained to me before looking back up at Arnold. 'How is Caroline feeling?'

The giant shrugged. 'She's doing well. Can't wait to come back and introduce everyone to the babies.'

'They just had twins!' Callie said fondly.

I nodded my greeting to the man and gazed over Callie's shoulder. Where were they keeping Damon?

'Are you OK?' Callie asked. She brushed my arm, and I flinched when the vervain touched my skin.

'I just need air,' I said, bursting out of the tent.

Callie ran after me. 'I'm sorry, Stefan,' she said, her voice cold. 'Some people don't like it here. They're not comfortable. But somehow I thought you'd be different.'

'No, it's not that.' Even surrounded by these human curiosities, I was the biggest freak of them all: the vampire who pretended to be human. 'I've just got a lot on my mind. I promise you, I like it here.'

'OK,' she said, not sounding quite convinced. But she continued to lead me farther into the grounds. We passed a two-headed cat, a sad-looking monkey playing 'Old Tom Dooley' on a harmonica, and the skeleton of what a sign declared to be a sea monster. Some freaks milling around were obviously actors, wearing fabric tubes filled with straw to simulate extra limbs, while others had been born that way.

'Come with me,' Callie said as she tugged on my arm. But I stayed. A black iron wagon rolled up to the tent, similar to the one Father had used to round up vampires during the Mystic Falls siege. It stopped, and the driver jumped from the cart. Immediately, five burly men rushed up with stakes. Once they were in place, the driver unlocked the back of the wagon. The scent of vervain wafted in the air, causing my joints to ache.

Damon.

'And there's your vampire,' Callie said, her mouth set in a firm line as all five men dragged Damon from the back of the wagon. One burly man, his sweat-stained shirt rolled at the sleeves, kept a stake positioned firmly over his heart.

'Gentle now, Jasper! We need him alive before the fight!' Callie called, her voice sharp. Damon turned, baring his teeth in our direction. I saw surprise in his eyes, which quickly turned into contempt.

'*My little brother, the good Samaritan*,' he whispered under his breath, barely moving his jaw. Luckily, he said it low enough that only I heard.

His voice sent a tremor through my body. Callie cocked her head, and I realized how risky it was for Damon and me to be in such close proximity. Would spite cause him to call me out as a fellow demon? 'Are you sure I can't help with the vampire?' I asked her.

'You heard my father. We'll start you at the ticket counter. And if anyone tries to sneak in, let Buck handle them,' she said, gesturing to the hulking man hovering several paces behind her like a distended shadow.

A commotion sounded in front of the tent. Callie let out a whistle as we approached. The front flap was closed tight, and a mass of people had surrounded a wooden ticket booth. Some, dressed in tattered breeches and with dirt-stained hands, were clearly from the shanty town surrounding the lake. But others were dressed in their finest: the men in top hats and silk smoking jackets, the women in feather-adorned hats and silk dresses, fur stoles draped around their bosoms.

Callie turned to me, her eyes shining. 'It's never been so busy. Dad's going to be so happy!' she said, clapping her hands together. 'Now, go help Buck,' she commanded before running back around the tent.

I stood in the wooden booth at the entrance, listening for Damon. But instead my ears filled with snatches of human conversation.

'I've got a hundred dollars on the lion.'

'No, the vampire. Monsters always win over beasts.'

'I've told this pretty lady here that she owes me a kiss if the beast wins.' One man hiccupped, obviously drunk.

I ground my teeth, wanting to lash out, to bite each and every one of them, to teach them a lesson. But I remembered Lexi's words about revenge. Killing these men would not help Damon.

A hand clapped my shoulder. I whirled around, ready to bare my teeth.

It was Gallagher, his face flushed with excitement. 'We have to hustle, son! The fight's about to start, and the more we pack 'em in, the bigger the payday.' He hopped on an overturned apple crate standing just outside the entrance.

'Step right up, folks! Welcome to my Odditorium! See the world's ugliest woman, marvel at the world's strongest man! But that's just the warm-up act. Because tonight, we have a battle royal, the likes of which have never been seen. Monster versus Beast. Who will win? And who wants to bet? Because this is one death that will lead to riches for some.'

The crowd pressed in more tightly around me, swarming like a mass of hungry insects.

Gallagher grinned at me. 'Get 'em in, and get 'em bidding.'

And so I held out my hand, collecting their coins and orange stubs of paper, all the while resisting the urge to reach out and snap their necks, as easily as I would a twig branch, and drink the liquid within.

CHAPTER 18

As soon as I'd taken every last ticket and accepted every last dollar, I slipped into the tent behind an overweight man clutching a sweaty wad of Confederate notes in each fist. The air was thick with the stench of sweat, sawdust, and of course, blood.

People were milling around us, paying extra money to gawk at the strong man and the tattooed lady, all of whom were hidden behind thick black curtains at various intervals along the perimeter of the tent. But the majority of the crowd was clamouring around Jasper. Large wagers were being placed, with lots of shouting and hand signals and stacks of greasy notes being passed back and forth. Jasper gleefully chomped on his soggy cigar and laughed.

Sailors yanked foreign bills from their billfolds. A few teenagers pooled their coins. Well-dressed men in ties waved gold coins.

'Fight, fight, fight!' one red-faced man began yelling. Instantly, the people standing by him began to chant as well. Three well-dressed women, their hair in curls atop their heads, glanced at each other, giggled, and echoed the cheer, their alto voices contrasting with the men's baritone ones.

Gallagher strode into the tent, his cane tapping a path through the sawdust. People turned and craned their necks to catch a glimpse of him; in the circus tent, he was just as much an attraction as the freaks. After all, this was the man who'd caught a vampire.

Be strong, brother, I whispered under my breath, remembering all the times Damon had won fights back in Mystic Falls. Damon had never provoked those battles but had always been a good fighter, always landing a punch fast when a fight broke out. That's why he'd been so respected in the army. But now, in a battle against a mountain lion, especially after not feeding for days . . . I shuddered.

'*Brother?*' I whispered tentatively, at a decibel I knew only his ears could detect. I was hoping for some sort of reply, even though I wasn't sure whether he could have actually heard me. If he did, he said nothing in response.

'And now, let's introduce our fighters!' Gallagher's voice broke through my reverie. Two animal handlers, their hands in leather gloves and wearing boots that came up past their knees, walked into the ring, leading a mangy mountain lion.

The mountain lion had a greyish-yellowish coat and yellow teeth, and, despite its lean body, looked brutal. And hungry. As if on cue, it uttered a roar.

'In one end of your ring, you have the mountain lion. But this is no ordinary cat. This beast is the Alberta Avenger! He came down from Canada to find the hunter that killed his mate. He eviscerated the hunter, his wife, and all of his children except the youngest, whose legs the lion ate before leaving the rest of him alive to tell the story. Since then, you have followed the mountain lion in the newspapers as it has feasted its way on innocents in the Union and Confederacy without prejudice. Tonight, it is here only after we captured it trying to stow away on a boat bound for the Andes Mountains in South America. The mountain lion, ladies and gentlemen!' Gallagher yelled, his showmanship on full display.

The crowd dutifully applauded enthusiastically, and some even cheered.

'Its opponent is a legendary vampire that has been terrifying children and their parents for centuries. Viktor the Cruel was born in 1589 and was heir to the Hapsburg Empire until he first tasted blood – his sister's – and began a three-hundred-year feeding frenzy that has left a trail of drained bodies around the world. At an estimated two victims per day, this brings Viktor's kills to one and a half million people, more than double the size of Italy. This unstoppable lust for blood continues tonight.'

The applause was more nervous now, but the cheers were louder.

Gallagher spread his hands apart with a flourish, and Damon came into the ring, surrounded by four handlers. His hands and feet were in chains, and his face was partially hidden by a muzzle. His skin was bleeding from the vervain, his eyes were bloodshot, and the expression on his face was one I'd never seen.

I could understand the hatred he felt – I was fighting every instinct I had not to kill the people holding him captive. But his imprisonment had changed him. Damon had called me a cold-blooded killer. The look in Damon's eyes was not one of sport, or survival. It was pure bloodlust.

A hush filled the tent. The mountain lion strained at his chains, but Damon simply stood in his corner of the ring, as if unaware of what the imminent future held for him.

'And . . . go!' Gallagher yelled. Immediately, the handlers unlocked Damon's chains and opened the iron door of the mountain lion's cage, then ran off the stage. The lion jumped towards Damon, making contact with his chest. Damon let out an anguished moan and fell backward. Then, just as quickly, he rose to his feet and roared, his face suddenly flushed, his fangs on full display. I knew this was all instinctual: Damon's Power rising to the surface as soon as he'd felt the attack. I had learned this about our kind in the past few weeks: our power led us to do things before we even knew we were doing them. Despite Damon's external weakness, his Power was still intact.

The lion leaped again, and Damon went low, ducking under the claws and coming up at just the right moment to dig his hands into the lion's neck. But the lion tossed Damon free; he rolled to a stop only when he slammed into the gate surrounding the ring.

Damon let out another moan and lay on the ground. The lion began to stalk over to claim his kill.

The crowd went wild, friends hitting one another in the arm and clawing at the air as though they themselves were in the fight.

One of the handlers positioned along the sidelines poked at Damon, clearly to get him moving. Damon swung without looking, knocking the man into the stands. As the handler struggled to get up, two nearby customers kicked him in the gut and then dropped him over the back railing to the dirt below, out of sight.

Damon paid no heed to the scuffle and moved deeper into the ring, letting the lion slowly circle him.

After a long silence, Damon let out a feral growl and ran towards the lion. The lion roared in response and charged, but this time Damon stepped aside, and when the lion missed him, Damon hooked an arm up under the lion's neck. With strength no one seemed to expect, Damon threw the lion onto its back. He was about to dive on top and go in for the kill when the lion kicked up and drove a claw right through Damon's arm.

The lion swatted its paw around, swinging Damon through the air like a fly on a fishing line. At last, the flesh gave way and Damon, with a red arc of blood trailing behind him, shot up through the air, then landed with a thud even I couldn't hear over the hellish roar of the celebrating crowd.

Damon struggled to his feet, holding the wounded arm in place with the other. He wasn't healing as quickly as vampires usually do – I wondered if the vervain had dampened that Power.

He needed blood, that much was clear. His survival instincts and the attendant adrenalin were waning. I was about to rush forward into the ring, with the stout man in front of me as an offering to my brother, when a warm hand fell on my arm.

Callie.

'It's horrible,' she said. Her knuckles had gone white around clumps of her dress. Her lips hung loose and trembled. 'I can't watch this barbarism much longer.'

'Then tell your father to stop it,' I hissed.

The stomping on the wooden stands was picking up in speed and along with the racing heartbeats of the people. The splotches of blood in the sawdust weren't enough to satisfy them – they needed to see a death.

Now Damon was padding around the mountain lion, as the animal hunched, coiled, in the centre of the ring, moving as little as possible while following Damon with its reflective eyes. Suddenly, Damon took off, moving at a blurred speed around the lion so that the animal had to rapidly turn and turn, as though chasing its own tail.

A quiet came over the crowd, and only the heavy panting of Damon and the mountain lion echoed under the canvas of the tent. Damon circled his prey, moving faster than the lion could comprehend.

The crowd gasped as Damon slanted towards the mountain lion, and before the beast could tell which direction he was coming from, Damon dived at the muscle behind the lion's head. He bit in and held on, letting the lion kick and flip wildly.

Callie clutched my arm. My eyes were riveted on the scene, and my body was primed to run to the cage should I need to intervene.

The mountain lion was slowing. Each time it bucked, more blood appeared in the sawdust in little red rivers. Its left hind leg was looking weak now; wobbling, it started to flop towards the ground. Damon unlatched his fangs and reared back, ready to go for the vein in the cat's neck.

Just then, the cat flailed its hindquarters and threw Damon free. As Damon tried to recover his feet, the mountain lion moved in and wrapped its jaws around his side.

The crowd gasped again, then began to boo.

Fight, I urged with every fibre of my being, clenching my fists at my sides.

Damon had gone limp and was being flung around like an old slipper in a dog's mouth. The lion tossed Damon to the ground, then pulled its head back and opened wide. But just as the animal dived forward, Damon rolled away. He drove his shoulder into the confused beast's side, bowling it over and exposing the short white hairs on its throat.

Damon tore into the vein with his fangs. The mountain lion twitched its way to stillness as a puddle of blood became bigger and bigger until it was a great lake of blood within the fighting ring. At its centre was my brother, kneeling over a dead mountain lion.

He stood and stumbled backward a step. He looked up into the crowd with a wide smile on his face, his fangs out and his whole face and front dripping with blood. The crowd cheered and booed in equal measure, and Damon just turned in a small circle, occasionally licking his lips.

Gallagher clapped his fat hands together. The ones who'd made money jumped and hugged one another. The ones who'd lost threw hats to the ground or stared blankly ahead.

I leaped forward, trying to push my way to my brother, but the handlers had already moved in, stakes and vervain-laced nets in hand. Damon was clearly drunk on such a massive feed after not eating for so long and didn't seem to notice them. Before I could even shout a warning, the men wrapped him in nets and began dragging him out of the arena.

Even at my fastest, I couldn't get past the crowd that had filled in behind them and now blocked the entire way. All of the revellers, hooting and slobbering, stood between me and the exit, and by the time I pushed and shoved my way out, the wagon was careening out of the fairgrounds.

A whip cracked. Hooves beat the ground. And just like that, Damon was gone.

CHAPTER 19

I ran past the shanties set up around the circus through the deep woods, following the tracks of the wagon until I lost the vehicle's scent completely at the outskirts of the city proper. A drunk was leaning against a brick building, whistling tunelessly.

In a blind rage, I roughly fell to my knees and grabbed him, biting into his neck and sucking his blood before he even had time to gasp. It tasted bitter, but I kept drinking, gulping it in until I could stand no more.

Sitting back on my heels, I wiped my mouth with the back of my hand, and looked around. Confusion and hatred coursed through my veins. Why couldn't I save Damon? Why had I just watched as Gallagher goaded the audience into placing even more bets, as the mountain lion pounced onto my brother? And why had Damon allowed himself to be captured and put me in this impossible position?

I wished I'd never insisted on turning him into a vampire in the first place. If he weren't here and I were alone in the city, everything would be so much easier. Now I was trying to be a good brother, and a good vampire, and yet was failing at everything.

I walked home, clomping up the steps to the house. I slammed the door, causing the hinges to rattle and one of the paintings in the parlour to fall on the floor with a clatter.

Instantly, I saw Buxton glaring at me from the opposite side of the room, his eyes glittering in the darkness. 'Is there some sort of problem you're having with the door?' he asked through clenched teeth.

I tried to brush past him, but he blocked my path.

'Excuse me,' I muttered, pushing him.

'Excuse you,' Buxton said, crossing his arms over his chest. 'Coming in as if you own the place. Stinking like humans. While I'm not one to question Miss Lexi, I do think it's time you showed a little respect for her home, brother.'

The word *brother* awakened something within me. 'Watch what you say,' I hissed, baring my teeth.

But Buxton just chuckled. 'I'll watch what I say when you watch how you act.'

'Boys?' Lexi called from upstairs, her lilting voice a contrast to the tense scene. She glided down the stairs, her eyes softening with concern when they rested on me. 'Is Damon . . . ?'

'He's alive,' I muttered. 'But I couldn't get to him.'

Lexi perched on the edge of a rickety rocking chair, her eyes large and sympathetic. 'Buxton, can you please get us some goat's blood?'

Buxton's eyes narrowed, but he shuffled out of the parlour and into the kitchen. In the living room, I could hear Hugo playing a lively French march on the piano.

'Thanks,' I said, sinking into an overstuffed love seat. I didn't want goat's blood. I wanted to gorge myself on gallons and gallons of human blood, drinking until I got sick and passed out in total oblivion.

'Remember, he's strong,' Lexi said.

'I'm not worried about Buxton,' I said.

'I meant your brother. If he's anything like you, he's strong.'

I looked up at her. She came over and took my chin in her hand.

'That's what you have to believe. It's what I believe. The trouble with you is that you want everything done right away. You're impatient.'

I sighed. The last thing I needed was another lecture about how I had no sense of the way the real vampire world worked.

Besides, I wasn't impatient. I was desperate.

'You just need to think of another plan. One we can help with.' Lexi glanced over as Buxton entered, carrying a silver tray laden with two mugs.

Buxton paused midstep. '*Faut-il l'aider?*' he asked in French.

'*Nous l'aiderons*,' Lexi replied.

Neither Lexi nor Buxton knew that I'd learned French at my mother's knee; it was odd to listen to them speak about whether to help me free Damon. I stared at my hands, which were still covered with crusted blood from my hunt earlier in the evening.

Buxton banged the tray against the polished cherrywood table. 'You will not put us in danger,' he growled, his fangs inches away from my neck. He shoved me with all his might against the wall, and the back of my head cracked against the fireplace's marble mantle.

My Power took over, and I pushed his shoulders hard. But Buxton was older and stronger than I was, and he kept me pinned to the wall, his hands firmly against my chest. I could feel blood beginning to seep from my skull, where I'd hit my head.

'You selfish, ungrateful monster,' Buxton whispered, hatred dripping from his voice. 'I've seen vampires like you before. You think the world is yours for the taking. You don't care about others. You don't care who you kill. You give us a bad name.'

I twisted and writhed, trying to escape his grip, when suddenly I felt the pressure release from my chest, followed by an enormous crash as Buxton fell to the floor.

'Buxton,' Lexi lectured, staring at the prone body lying at her feet. 'How many more centuries will it be before you learn how to treat a guest? And, Stefan, won't you agree with me that human blood simply doesn't agree with you? That behaviour wasn't necessary.' Lexi shook her head like an annoyed schoolmarm. 'Now, I'll drink my blood in peace. Be nice, boys,' she said as she glided out of the room, the mug of blood in her hands.

How could she walk away so casually, knowing that my brother was out there imprisoned and tortured? I had come to depend on Lexi for many things, and support in finding and saving Damon was my only priority now.

As if reading my mind, she paused at the archway to her quarters, glancing from one of us to the other. 'If and when I say we help Damon, we will. Is that clear to both of you?'

'Yes, Miss Lexi,' Buxton murmured as he slowly eased onto his knees then stood up.

I nodded, barely containing my scowl. *If?*

Buxton limped out of the room, but not before he threw one last glare in my direction.

Suddenly the house felt too small, as though the walls, floors and ceilings were pressing in at me from all sides. Letting out one last growl, I flew through the parlour, out the door, and back down to Lake Road.

CHAPTER 20

The next morning, I woke as someone shook my shoulder.

'Go away,' I murmured. But the shaking was insistent.

My eyes snapped open, and I realized I was lying curled up next to one of the tents at Gallagher's freak show.

'Did you sleep here?' Callie asked, crossing her arms over her chest. I sat up, rubbing the sleep from my eyes, thinking about the previous evening. I'd returned to the circus grounds, unsure of where else to go and had fallen asleep there.

'Good morning, Miss Callie,' I said, ignoring her question. I stood up and brushed dirt off the back of my trousers. 'How can I help you?'

She shrugged. She was clad in a pink cotton dress that showed her tiny waist and freckled arms. The colour stood in contrast to her flowing red hair, and she reminded me of a wild rose. 'We're going to take a few days off from the show.

Father made so much money, he wants the next event to be even bigger.' Callie smiled. 'The first rule of show business: keep 'em wanting more.'

'How's Da— the vampire?' I asked, shielding my eyes from the sun. While my ring protected me from the agony of the rays, the sun made me feel exposed and clumsy. The dark cloaked more than my fangs, and in the light of day, I constantly had to check to make sure I wasn't moving at lightning speed, responding to questions I shouldn't be able to hear, or following my urge to feed.

Callie tucked a loose strand of rust-coloured hair behind her ear. 'The vampire is OK, I suppose. Father has its handlers tending to it around the clock. They don't want it to die. Not yet, anyway.'

Not yet was a small comfort, but it was something. It meant I still had time.

She frowned slightly. 'Of course, I hardly think they should let it die at all. What we're doing to it, and to the animals it fights, is totally barbaric,' she said softly, almost speaking to herself.

I looked up swiftly at the words. Was she more sympathetic to Damon's plight than I'd imagined? 'Can I see him?' I asked, surprised at my boldness.

Callie swatted my arm. 'No! Not unless you pay up, like everyone else. Besides, he's not here.'

'Oh.'

'Oh,' she said, mocking me. Then her eyes softened. 'I still can't believe you slept here. Don't you have a home?'

I met her gaze straight on. 'I had . . . a disagreement with my family.' It wasn't exactly a lie.

The freak show was starting to wake up. The strong man walked, bleary-eyed, out of a tent. Abruptly, he dropped down to the ground and began doing push-ups. The fortune-teller headed to the secluded part of the lake, towel in hand, no doubt for a bath. And two of the ever-present burly security men were watching Callie and me curiously.

Callie clearly noticed as well. 'Would you like to go for a walk?' she asked, leading the way down a dirt-packed road to the edge of the lake, out of sight of the show. She picked up a stone and threw it into the water, where it landed with a thunk.

'I never could skip stones,' she said, in such a sad voice that I couldn't help but burst out laughing.

'What's so funny?' she asked, hitting my arm again. The swat was playful, but the bracelets she wore were twisted through with vervain, and the contact sent a wave of pain up my arm. She put her hand on my shoulder, concern creasing her forehead. 'Are you OK?'

I winced. 'Yes,' I lied.

'OK . . .' she said, throwing me a sceptical look. She

leaned down to pick up another stone and raised her light brown eyebrow at me before she threw it in the water. It fell with a harmless *plop*.

'Tragic!' I picked up my own stone and aimed it across the water. It skipped five times before falling below the surface.

Callie laughed and clapped her hands. 'You must teach me!'

'You have to flick your wrist. And pick a flat stone.' I spotted a smooth brown rock with a white band ringing the top. 'Here.' I put the rock in her hands. 'Now, flick,' I said, gingerly touching her skin, making sure my fingers didn't brush against the vervain.

She closed her eyes and tossed the stone, which skipped once, before falling into the water. She threw her arms up in delight. 'Thank you, Stefan,' she said, her eyes twinkling.

'No more "stranger"?' I teased.

'You've taught me something. That means we're friends.'

'Does it, now?' I said, taking another stone and tossing it in the water. Damon and I had skipped stones in the pond near our home in Mystic Falls. We'd make wishes and pretend that they would come true if we could guess the number of skips a stone would make.

I closed my eyes briefly. *If it skips five times, I'll have a chance to free Damon*, I thought. But this stone was heavier and sank after two skips. I shook my head, annoyed at myself for indulging in such a childish game.

'So was that your biggest concern in the world? That you couldn't skip stones?' I teased, trying to reclaim the light tone of our outing.

She smiled, but her eyes looked sad. 'No. But don't you think pretend problems are much more manageable than real ones?'

'Yes, I do,' I said quietly.

The sun was steadily rising, lending the lake an orange glow. Several small skiffs were already on the water, casting their nets, and the wind whipped around our ears, a reminder that even though the sun felt warm, winter was well on its way.

'I've never talked to anyone about this. That's rule number two of the Gallagher family business – don't trust anyone,' she said.

'Your father seems tough,' I ventured, sensing her frustration. 'Perhaps too tough?'

'My father is fine,' Callie snapped. She scowled at me, hands on her hips.

'I'm sorry,' I said, raising my hands in surrender. I realized I'd pushed too far too quickly. 'That was out of line.'

Callie let her hands fall to her sides. 'No, I'm sorry. I'm just protective of him. He's all I have.'

'Where is your mother?' I asked.

'Died when I was six,' Callie said simply.

'I understand,' I said, thinking of my own mother. 'It's hard, isn't it?'

Callie plucked a blade of grass from the ground and shredded it between her fingernails. 'I try to be strong. But after Mother died, Father threw himself into work.'

'It seems that you do that as well.'

'Now that Father's got the vampire act worked out, I feel like things will change for the better. He has a short fuse that gets shorter the less money he has.'

At the mention of the vampire act, I kicked the stones around the edge of the shore. A flurry of pebbles flew through the air and landed several metres into the lake with a violent splashing sound.

'What was that?' Callie asked, alarm in her voice.

I forced myself to smile, to look calm – human. In my anger, I'd forgotten to hide my Power. 'Advanced stone skipping.'

Callie raised an eyebrow, as if she wanted to challenge me. But all she said was: 'We should get back. Dad wants us to clean up the grounds.'

I nodded. 'Good idea.' Alone here with Callie, I'd come so close to losing control.

'Stefan,' Callie said. 'I was thinking . . . since we don't

have the shows for a few nights, do you think you could show me the city?'

'But I don't know the city,' I pointed out. 'You've been here longer than I have.'

Callie's cheeks flushed poppy red. 'Father doesn't let me leave the house, unless it's for work. But there are so many shows and adventures in New Orleans.' She looked up at me from beneath her long lashes. 'Please? I'll feel safe if I'm with you.'

I nearly laughed at the irony of that statement, but the chuckle caught in my throat. Callie had it wrong: she wouldn't necessarily be safe with me, but I could use her to guarantee the safety of my brother. After all, she knew everything about Gallagher's Circus – including where her father was holding Damon.

'OK, let's do it,' I said.

'Oh, we'll have such fun!' Callie clasped my hands and whirled me around. 'Meet me at the park at the end of my street at nine o'clock.' She rose onto her tiptoes and kissed my cheek.

She was so close, I could practically feel her heart beating against my chest. I pulled away abruptly, my head pounding and my jaw aching. I turned my back to her as my canines extended with a click. I had to take five deep breaths before they retracted again.

'Are you OK?' she asked, placing her hand on my shoulder.

I plastered a smile on my face and turned back to her. 'Just excited for tonight.'

'Good,' Callie said, humming to herself as we walked back to the circus grounds.

I ran my tongue over my teeth. It was true: I was excited for tonight. But excitement was akin to desire, and as I'd been learning ever since I met Katherine, nothing good ever came from desire.

CHAPTER 21

I arrived at home at dusk and found Lexi perched on the couch, her arms folded over her chest, and her foot rapidly tapping the floor. She looked like a disgruntled mother hen. Hugo and Percy were lounging, cat-like, on chaises in the far corner. Buxton, I noted with relief, was nowhere to be seen. I wondered how long they'd been waiting for me.

'You decided to come back, I see,' Lexi said, a scowl crossing her face.

'So I did,' I said, trying to suppress a smile.

'And something's changed,' she added. She sniffed the air. 'But you haven't fed, that's good.' She knitted her eyebrows together.

'Hello,' I said to Hugo and Percy, ignoring Lexi's observation. They gazed at me in surprise. I'd never made any effort to speak to either of them in the past.

'Hi,' Percy grunted.

Hugo just stared at me.

Lexi continued to glare at me, her hands on her hips. 'Out with it, Stefan. We don't keep secrets in this house.'

'I have a plan to free Damon,' I said, wincing at the giddy sound of my voice.

'That's terrific!' Lexi clapped. 'How are you going to do it?'

'Well, uh, it begins with going on a date,' I confessed.

'A date?' Lexi's brows flew up. 'With whom?'

I cleared my throat sheepishly. 'With Gallagher's daughter, Callie.'

'You have a date with a *human*?!' Percy said just as Lexi blurted out, 'You have a date with *Callie Gallagher*.'

I put my hands up defensively. 'She wants me to take her out on the town tonight. And while we're there, I'm going to get information out of her on Damon. I can't influence her because of the vervain, but there are other ways to get a woman to talk.'

Percy and Hugo looked up, expressions of disapproval crossing their faces like thunderclouds.

'I wouldn't do that if I were you,' Hugo said. I glanced at him in surprise. Apart from the night they'd found me, it was the first time I'd ever heard him speak.

'I agree. You'll either want to kill her or kiss her, and neither scenario will end well for you,' Percy said. The sentence sounded out of place coming from his scrawny, baby-faced body.

'They're right,' Lexi said urgently. 'They've learned their lessons the hard way. Who's to say what you'll do when you're alone with that girl, not to mention what she'll do to you. You saw her house . . . the weapons she has. I just worry that—'

'I know, I know. I'm young, I can't control my impulses, and I'm going to make some sort of mistake,' I interrupted in annoyance.

Lexi stood up and gazed at me. 'All of those things are true. You're strong, but I worry that you might let your emotions get the better of you.'

'I won't,' I protested. 'I'm just going out with her to see if I can learn anything more about Damon. If I'm going to rescue him – peacefully – she's my best bet.'

Lexi set her jaw, but then heaved a sigh. 'Just be careful.'

'If you're going out, you can't wear that,' Hugo said, lumbering up from the chaise. 'Percy, get him something nice to wear.'

Percy looked at Lexi beseechingly. She crossed her arms. 'What? You heard the man.'

Percy slid off the couch and marched up the stairs.

'If you're going out with a lady, you need to look nice,'

Hugo explained gruffly. 'And Lexi, you need to take him shopping.'

'Yes, we'll go out tomorrow night, Stefan,' she replied.

'Why are you suddenly being so helpful?' I asked Hugo suspiciously.

Hugo showed his pointy teeth in a small smile. 'If you free Damon with the human's help, there'll be no need for us to get involved. Now, go get dressed!'

I rolled my eyes but followed Percy up the stairs. He handed me a white linen shirt and a pair of black trousers.

For a moment I wished that I had brand-new clothes and pomade to slick my hair back with. But then I reminded myself of what I'd told Lexi: right now, I just had to focus on getting to know Callie Gallagher, and, subsequently, learn what made Patrick Gallagher tick.

But even though I kept telling myself that Damon was my reason for going on this date, I couldn't help but notice that my mind kept drifting back to the moment when Callie kissed my cheek.

CHAPTER 22

I straightened the cuffs on my neatly pressed white shirt and buttoned my overcoat. The shiny brass buttons glinted in the lamplight as I turned the corner onto Laurel Street.

I wiped my face, to make sure no blood lingered on my lips. I'd visited my barmaid from Miladies, sating my hunger before my evening out on the town with Callie. The barmaid's blood had tasted sweet, like lilies dipped in honey. The second the warmth had hit my tongue, my senses had become honed and the world had sharpened around the edges.

Now the cicadas shrieked in my ears and the smell of roses assaulted my nose, but my stomach was calm and my veins were sated. I was ready for my date.

The park at the end of the street was filled with magnolias and ancient elm trees, and in the centre, a marble fountain was topped with a sculpture of a naked woman. Through the burble of the fountain, I could hear the beating of a human heart.

'Hello?' I called.

'Stefan!' Callie stepped out from behind a stone cherub into the weak light of a gas lamp. Her red hair, a flame in the flickering light, hung loose and curly around her shoulders. She wore a simple, cream-coloured dress, with a lace bodice and a flouncy skirt that draped over her tiny hips.

Blood raced through my body.

'What?' Callie said, reddening as she noticed my stare.

'You look, uh, like a girl,' I said. She looked beautiful.

'Gee, thanks.' Callie rolled her eyes and softly slugged my shoulder. 'You're just used to seeing me in work clothes.' She gazed at me. 'You look quite handsome.'

I cleared my throat and tugged on my collar. Suddenly my clothes felt uncomfortable and constricting, and the night air stuffy. I wondered briefly if the barmaid had something in her blood that hadn't agreed with me. 'Thank you,' I said formally.

'Stefan?' Callie lifted her arm expectantly.

'Oh, of course.' I took her arm in mine. Her freckled hand grazed my palm. I flinched and readjusted so that her hand was resting on the soft fabric of my jacket.

'Where to, Miss Gallagher?'

She looked up at me, a smile on her face. 'Bourbon Street, of course.'

Callie guided me through cobblestone side streets, where gardenias dripped from balconies. On a whim, I grabbed one and tucked it behind her ear. Back home in Mystic Falls, it was customary to bring flowers or a small token when visiting with a lady.

'Want to know a secret?' Callie whispered.

'What?' I asked, curious. I was already the bearer of too many secrets. But perhaps Callie's could lead me to Damon . . .

She got up on tiptoe and cupped my ear with her hand. The sound of her blood pumping beneath her skin magnified tenfold. I gritted my teeth, forcing my fangs back down. 'Your shirt has come untucked,' she whispered.

'Oh,' I said, as I self-consciously smoothed down my shirt. 'Thanks.'

Callie let out a gleeful laugh. 'You know what I really want to see?' she asked, grabbing my arm.

'What?' I asked, trying to devote all my energy to not listening to the steady thrum of her blood.

'A burlesque show. Madame X has a show *everyone's* been talking about,' she said.

We walked together through the town, past bustling crowds and wavering street carts, ending up in a well-kept neighbourhood in front of a pristine, stately house. A simple placard next to the door read MADAME X in black script. Soft lamplight shone from all the windows, and carriages pulled up, one after another, to the front gate, releasing their well-dressed passengers into the depths of the club.

I momentarily panicked. I didn't have any money. And I was wearing a schoolboy's clothes that hadn't been in style since the turn of the century.

'Callie, I think . . .' I began, trying to come up with an alternate idea for our evening when the front door swung open to greet us.

'Good evening. Are you guests of the house?' The man's eyes flicked down my old clothes. I was wildly underdressed for this venue, and I knew it. Callie, however, looked radiant.

'Yes,' Callie jumped in, straightening her shoulders.

'And your names?'

From the way Callie's lips flattened, I could tell she hadn't realized there was a guest list. I stepped in front of her, suddenly inspired. 'We're the Picards. Remy and his wife, Calliope.'

'One moment, sir.' The man waddled in his slippers over to a podium holding a list that almost certainly did not include Mr Remy Picard's name. He turned a page, then turned it back.

'What are you doing, Stefan?' Callie whispered.

'I have it under control,' I said quietly. 'Just smile and look pretty.'

The man returned, looking genuinely distressed.

'I'm terribly sorry, sir, but your name is not on our list for tonight.' He glanced around, as if ready to beckon a security guard if we made trouble.

I want you to let us in without asking us any more questions, I thought, channeling all my energy. 'We'd really like to come in,' I said aloud, concentrating on looking deep into his eyes, ignoring Callie's curious gaze boring into my back. 'Are you sure you didn't see our names on the list?'

The man's eyes flickered.

Let us in without looking at the list.

'You know, I believe I *might* have seen your names. In fact, I'm sure I did. The Picards! I'm sorry. It was my confusion. Right this way,' he said, a slightly vacant expression on his face. He led us through large double doors and into a sumptuous parlour. Low crystal chandeliers hung from the ceiling, and the air smelled of jasmine, magnolia, and freesia.

'Enjoy your stay at Madame X's. And if I can be of any assistance to either of you, don't hesitate to come fetch me,' the man said, turning on his heel.

'Thank you,' I said.

Callie simply stood there, looking slack-jawed at me. 'How did you do that?'

I shrugged. 'I just made him doubt himself. He wouldn't want to say no to the Picards, whoever they are. Besides, what if our names *were* on the list, and he said no to us, then we complained to the owner?' Secretly, I was thrilled. My Power was strengthening.

'So I take it that this isn't your first time sneaking in where you don't belong?'

I glanced at her slyly. 'You of all people should know that to be true.'

She laughed, and I gave her an impromptu twirl. People stared at us. Even though a pianist was playing a jaunty tune in the corner, this wasn't a room where people danced. Instead, guests drifted from one conversation to the next as they sucked on cigars and gulped down champagne.

'Do you know anyone here?' I asked as we brushed past couple after couple, all clad in finery.

Callie shrugged, the shadow of a frown crossing her face. She glanced around the room. 'They all hate Father. They say he's a Unionist who's taking advantage of New Orleans with his business. And perhaps he is, but at least his show doesn't pretend to be something it's not,' she said, jutting her chin.

I shifted in my seat. Wasn't that exactly what I was doing? Pretending to be someone I wasn't? I couldn't look at her, in case she could see the depths of my lies in my eyes.

A server came by with a tray laden with champagne. I grabbed two glasses.

'Cheers,' I said, handing one to Callie.

As we sipped the bubbling liquid, conversations swirled around us, growing louder and more boisterous with every tray of drinks the waiters brought out to serve. Men's movements grew more languid, women laughed more readily.

'Is your father ready for the next show?' I asked, forcing a conversational note to my voice.

'I suppose so.'

'Who will the vampire be fighting?'

'I don't know,' Callie said. 'A crocodile, or maybe a tiger. It depends on what Father can get on such short notice. Why?'

I shrugged non-committally. 'I want to place a bet.'

'Father wants something cheap. He's worried people won't pony up as much money for another animal fight. It seems the monster's much stronger than a beast.'

'Oh,' I said, trying to process the information.

'But let's not talk about work. Tonight is supposed to be fun! Lord knows we don't have enough of it in our real lives.' Callie's voice grew melancholy. 'Speaking of fun,' she said, pointing to a small crowd moving through a set of double doors at the back of the club, 'I think the burlesque show is back there.'

'Shall we?' I asked, offering my arm.

The back room, much smaller than the first one, had numerous wooden tables crammed onto the floor. A stage was set up at the front of the room, and the space was dimly lit by candles. Instead of joining the crush towards the front, Callie and I sat back on a low-slung, red velvet bench beneath a large mirror in the back of the room.

As soon as everyone settled into seats, a master of ceremonies took to the stage. I was surprised to see that he was a man wearing a dinner suit and cape. I'd imagined a burlesque show to be louder, larger than this, with plenty of music and scantily clad women.

'Good evening! As we've all heard, we have a vampire in our midst,' he said dramatically.

Audience members tittered nervously. I glanced at Callie out of the corner of my eye. Was this some sort of trap? Did she know what I was? But Callie was leaning forward, as if mesmerized by the man's words.

The master of ceremonies smiled, drinking in the suspense. 'Yes, a vampire. Down at that two-bit circus by the lake.'

Jeers filled the room. Callie hadn't been exaggerating when she'd said her father was infamous in this town.

I turned to look at her. Although her cheeks were as red as her hair, she gazed straight ahead, her elbows on her knees.

'And eyewitnesses say Gallagher had to chain his up so it won't run away. But, here at Madame X's, our vampire has come to visit all on his own.'

'We can go if you want,' I whispered.

But Callie shook her head and clasped my hand. It felt warm against my cool skin, but this time I didn't push her away. 'No, I want to stay.'

A thin man walked onstage, clad in a black cape. His face was powdered, and thin lines of fake blood were drawn from the corners of his lips. He smiled at the crowd, revealing fake fangs. I shifted in my seat.

'I am a vampire, and you all are my prey! Come to me, my pretties!' he cackled, in an exaggerated voice that made me squirm. The 'vampire' stalked around the stage, his teeth bared and his eyes scanning the audience. A woman in a pearl-embroidered gown stood up from a table in the front and walked towards the stage as if in a trance, emitting a low moan with each step.

'The vampire has special eyes that can see through clothing. And this vampire, ladies and gentlemen, likes what he sees!' The master of ceremonies leered at the audience.

At this, the audience applauded enthusiastically.

I glanced at Callie again. Had she known this was a show about vampires?

'But, now, the vampire has his hunger awakened. And what he'll do to feed the hunger, you won't believe,' the master of ceremonies said as the vampire onstage waved his hands towards the woman, as if conducting an orchestra. As he did that, a trumpet player began playing a slow, mournful tune. The woman began to move her hips, slowly at first, and then more and more quickly until she looked as though she would topple over.

'Maybe Father should give our vampire dance lessons,' Callie whispered, her breath hot on my cheek.

Then, suddenly, the vampire stopped waving his arms. The music stopped, and so did the woman. The vampire lurched towards her, took hold of the sleeve of her dress, and tore it off, exposing her milky-white arm.

'Do you feel wicked tonight?' the vampire called to the audience, waggling the fabric towards the crowd. Then he tore off the other sleeve.

My stomach turned.

'I ask you, do you feel wicked tonight?' he called again, tossing the fabric into the audience.

The crowd cheered as the dancer continued her gyrations, rubbing her back against the 'vampire'. Slowly, she peeled away her clothing, item by item, sending a silk stocking or a slip into the audience until most of her body was on display.

As the music picked up speed, she got closer to becoming entirely nude. At last, she sat in a chair on the stage as the master of ceremonies pulled off the last bit of her top, forcing her to cover herself with her hands.

'As he is a beast from hell, the only way to stop a vampire is with a stake to the heart. But they can also be kept away with a crucifix . . .'

At this, the dancer pantomimed a futile search for pockets that might contain a stake or crucifix.

I slumped in my chair, thinking of my own attacks. Of Alice, of Lavinia, of the nurse whose name I'd never known. There was nothing beautiful or romantic about those attacks. They were quick, bloody, deadly. I'd ended their lives without a second thought, with swift violence and a thirst for more.

'Are you OK?' Callie asked.

For the first time, I realized how tightly I'd been clutching her hand. I loosened my grip, and instantly she snuggled closer to me in my seat. Her blood pumped like sweet music through her body, and the warmth of her body soothed my anger. I relaxed into her, taking in the softness of her voice as she laughed at the play. Callie was warm and soft and so very *alive*. I wanted this moment to freeze, to last into eternity, with nothing but me and Callie and her beating heart. There was nothing else I needed in that moment, not blood, not power, not D—

My body tensed and I sat straight up. What was I doing? Had I forgotten my brother, what I had done to him, so quickly?

I stood up.

'Down in front!' a voice barked a few rows behind me.

'I-I'm sorry. I have to go,' I said, stumbling towards the door.

'Stefan, wait!' she called.

But I kept going until I was on the street, running from the late-night bustle all the way to the riverbank. As I stared down at my reflection in the swirling water, Percy's words echoed in my head: 'You'll either want to kill her or kiss her, and neither scenario will end well for you.'

He was right. Because while I truly didn't know whether I wanted to kiss or bite Callie, I knew I wanted *her*.

CHAPTER 23

October 9, 1864

I am not supposed to have a heart. A bullet went through it nearly three weeks ago, and no blood of my own will ever pump through it again. The only blood that now courses through my veins is that of whomever I happen to attack. And yet something about Callie causes my dead heart to flutter and the stolen blood to quicken in my body.

Is it real? Or is it a mere memory of something that used to be? Damon once told me that on the battlefield, boys who'd undergone amputations still woke up to agonizing pain in their legs or cried for the hand that ached, though those limbs were no longer part of them. But while those boys had phantom limbs, it seems I have a phantom heart.

In my short time in New Orleans, I've learned about

my Power. It's what has driven me, what I've thrived on, what makes me a vampire. But that's not the only power I possess. The other kind isn't exciting, or thrilling, or dangerous. It's mundane and tedious – the exercising of control over my Power. I've had to learn to suppress my urges to fit in and to remain with Lexi.

Yet when I was with Callie at the show, it was as though my two powers were at cross-purposes, each threatening to destroy the other in a private battle in my brain.

Now she enters my thoughts constantly. The constellation of freckles on her skin. Her long eyelashes. Her vibrant smile. I can't help but admire the way she wields her own power. How she commands the attention and respect of her father's employees, but also how she grows soft around me, cuddling close when she thinks no one is looking.

I think of my hand interlaced with hers.

And every time an image of Callie floats to my consciousness, I curse myself. I should be stronger than this. I shouldn't think of her. I should put her out of my mind, write her off as a silly little girl who is lucky I'm letting her live.

But deep down, despite my Power, I know Callie has control over me – and my phantom heart.

The next morning, I returned to the freak show, with only one thing on my mind: freeing Damon.

'Hello, friend!' the strong man, Arnold, greeted me as I walked through the gateway to the fairgrounds.

'Hello,' I muttered.

The tattooed woman came up behind him and gazed at me quizzically. Without her India-inked designs, she was actually quite pretty, with high cheekbones and wide, inquisitive eyes. 'What are you doing here?'

I grunted in response.

'You'll want to apologize to Callie.' She pointed at the side of the tent.

So Callie had already told her friends about our disastrous evening. Just as I had feared. I walked around the grounds until I saw Callie kneeling over a piece of birch wood at her feet. Paint splattered her overalls, and her red hair was twisted on top of her head and held in place by a single, slender, long-handled paintbrush. The sign said:

A PENNY A PEEK: A REAL, LIVE, HUNGRY VAMPIRE. ENTER IF YOU DARE!

Underneath was a crude drawing of a vampire: fangs elongated, eyes squinting, blood trickling down both sides of his mouth. The features were Damon's, but it was clear Callie had drawn significant artistic inspiration from the burlesque show last night.

Callie looked up, catching me staring. Her mouth made a round O, and she dropped her brush onto the canvas. A large black spot suddenly appeared on Damon's face.

'Look what you made me do,' she said angrily.

I stuck my hands in my pockets, subtly sniffing the air for traces of Damon. 'I'm sorry.'

Callie sighed in annoyance. 'I don't need your apologies. I just need you to stop distracting me so I can get some work done.'

'Do you want me to help you fix the painting?' The words were out of my mouth before I could stop them. They hung between us for a long moment, both of us seemingly surprised by my offer.

'Fix the painting?' Callie echoed, putting her hands on her hips. 'Am I hearing you correctly? Fix the *painting*?'

'Yes?' I fumbled.

'Are you aware that you left me last night to get home alone, with no explanation?' Her chin was jutted out, and her stance was aggressive, but her lower lip wobbled, and I could tell she was hurt.

'Callie,' I began. Excuses flew through my head. *I work for your father. We should not sneak around. You're just a girl, and I'm a vampire . . .* Even though part of me was furious at her for allowing her father to parade Damon around like livestock, to let him fight perhaps until death, the other part knew that she had as little sway over her father as I'd had with mine. And now all I could think about was making her lip stop wobbling.

'It's better this way,' I said, twisting my ring around my finger.

She shook her head and stabbed the sharp wooden end of the paintbrush into the dirt. It remained there, as if it were a tiny surrender flag after a battle. 'No explanation necessary. We've known each other a week. You don't owe me an explanation. That's the best thing about strangers: you don't owe them anything,' she said crisply.

I rocked back on my heels. A silence hung between us. The image of Damon glared up at me, seemingly mocking my ineffectiveness.

'Well, aren't you going to get to work?' she asked. 'Or are we just paying you to stand around?'

Before I could turn to leave, Jasper burst out of a small black tent at the edge of the property. 'We need some extra hands!'

A lanky man trailed behind him, cradling his forearm close to his chest.

Callie leaped to her feet. 'What happened?'

As the man held out his hand, blood flowed down his arm onto the ground. I averted my eyes. Even so, pain rippled along my jaw as I felt my fangs grow.

'The vampire's fighting today. We need more men,' Jasper gasped breathlessly, his eyes falling on me.

'Stefan,' Callie said in a tone that wasn't a question.

Jasper and the stocky man stared at me.

'Well then, come on, new guy. Show us you're Gallagher material,' Jasper said, jerking his chin in the direction of the tent.

'Of course,' I said slowly, a plan forming in my mind. I could pick out four separate heartbeats in the tent. There would be copious amounts of vervain, of course, but I'd been feeding regularly enough that I might be able to overcome the men. Four I could handle, but five . . . I turned to Jasper. 'Why don't you and Callie take care of your man here and I'll join the others in the tent?'

'*I'm coming, brother*,' I added under my breath.

Callie squinted at me. 'Did you say something?'

'No,' I said quickly.

Jasper shifted from foot to foot, sizing me up with his eyes. 'Callie will take care of Charley here, and I'll take care of you. Teach you the tricks of monster wrangling,' he said, clapping me on the back, pushing me towards the tent.

With each step the scent of vervain grew stronger, curdling the blood in my veins.

Together, we entered the tent. The interior was hot and dark, the stench of vervain nearly suffocating me. It took every ounce of my strength not to bend at the waist and scream in agony. I forced my eyes open and looked at my brother, who was chained in the corner. Four men yanked on his restraints, trying desperately to keep him in place.

The second Damon's eyes landed on me, his face lit up.

'*Welcome to hell, brother*,' Damon whispered, his lips barely moving as he locked eyes with me. Then he turned to Jasper. 'So, Jasp,' he said, in a conversational tone, as if they were just two men engaged in a friendly talk at a tavern, 'you found a new sap to do your dirty work. Well, come on, brother. Let's see if you can stake me.'

'His bark is worse than his bite,' Jasper said, holding out a stake to me. From its stench I could tell it had been soaked in vervain.

'Give me your gloves,' I said with an air of authority. Touching the wood would give me away instantly.

'Won't give you much protection. Those fangs can go through anything,' Jasper protested.

'Just give them to me,' I said through clenched teeth. Damon watched the exchange intently, clearly enjoying my predicament.

'OK, if they'll make you more comfortable . . .' Jasper shrugged and handed me his leather gloves. I pulled them over my hands and took the stake from Jasper, my hands trembling slightly. How could something so light be so deadly?

Damon let out a low chuckle. 'Is this the best you could rustle up? He looks about ready to keel over.'

I glared at my brother. '*I'm trying to save you*,' I whispered.

Damon just snorted derisively.

'*Please*,' I added.

'*Please what?*' he said, wrapping the chains around his hands.

'*Please let me save you*.'

'*Sorry. Can't help you there*,' he said, before yanking on the chains. Two of the guards fell to the ground in surprise.

'Do something!' Jasper said gruffly. 'You've got to stick him, let him know his place.'

'*Listen to your boss*,' Damon sneered. '*Be a man and stab me. A real man isn't afraid of blood, isn't that right?*'

Jasper bent down and grabbed a stake from the ground.

'C'mon, boy. Earn your keep,' he said, using the side of the stake to nudge me forward. I gasped. Pain shot up and down my skin, as if I'd been touched by a hot poker.

Damon laughed again.

The flap opened, and Callie poked her head through the tent.

I looked wildly over at her. 'Callie, you shouldn't be here!'

Both she and Damon looked at me quizzically. A sickening feeling spread through my limbs. The vervain, the heat, the stakes . . .

Just then, with a simple twist from his chains, Damon broke free and lunged towards Callie. Callie shrieked, and Jasper dived to shield her.

Time seemed to stop, and without thinking, I hurled my stake through Damon's belly. He fell backward, gasping, blood spurting from the wound.

'I said, please!' I hissed wildly, in a voice only Damon could hear. Callie cowered near the flap, her eyes wide as she glanced between me and Damon.

Damon looked up, wheezing as he pulled the stake from his stomach. Then I heard the faintest, hoarse whisper over the shouts of Jasper and the trainers as they moved to re-chain Damon.

'Then please know that your hell hasn't even yet begun, brother.'

CHAPTER 24

I ran down to the lake, the sound of the stake ripping through Damon's flesh echoing in my mind. Once I got to the shore, I stared at my reflection in the water. My hazel eyes stared back, my lips pressed into a thin line. With an angry jerk, I threw a pebble into the pond, shattering my image into a thousand little ripples.

Part of me wanted to jump in the lake, swim to the other side, and never come back. Damn Damon to hell if death was what he wanted so much. But no matter how much I wished he'd die, I couldn't kill him. Despite everything, we were brothers, and I wanted – *needed* – to do everything in my power to save him. After all, blood was thicker than water. I laughed bitterly as I thought of the deeper meanings of the metaphor. Blood was also more complicated, more destructive, and more heartbreaking than water.

I sank into the brackish sand at the water's edge and lay

back with a sigh, letting the wan November sun cascade over me. I don't know how long I remained like that before I felt muffled footfalls vibrate the ground beneath me.

I sighed. I don't know what I'd hoped to find, coming down to the lake, but my peace and quiet was ruined when Callie sat down next to me.

'Everything OK?' she asked, throwing a small rock into the lake with a *plunk*. She didn't turn to face me.

'I just . . . could you leave me alone?' I muttered. 'Please.'

'No.'

I sat up and looked her square in the face. 'Why not?'

Callie pursed her lips, her forehead crinkling as though she were working through a complicated problem. Then, hesitantly, she reached out with her tiny pinky finger and traced the outline of my lapis lazuli ring.

'The monster has a ring like this,' she said.

I jerked my hand away in horror. How could I have forgotten about our rings?

Callie cleared her throat. 'Is the vampire, is he your . . . brother?'

My blood ran cold, and I jumped to my feet.

'No, Stefan! Stay.' Callie's green eyes were wide, her cheeks flushed. 'Please. Just stay. I know what you are, and I'm not afraid.'

I took a step back, my breath coming in rapid gasps. My

mind spun, and I felt nauseated all over again. 'How can you know what I am and not fear me?'

'You're not a monster,' she said simply. She rose to her feet as well.

For a moment, we just stood there, not speaking, barely breathing. A duck cut an arc through the lake. A horse whinnied in the distance. And the scent of pine tickled my nose. I noticed then that Callie had removed all the vervain from her hair.

'How can you say that?' I asked. 'I could kill you in an instant.'

'I know.' She looked into my eyes as if searching for something. My soul, perhaps. 'So why haven't you? Why don't you now?'

'Because I like you,' I said, surprising myself with the words.

A whisper of a smile flitted across her lips. 'I like you too.'

'Are you sure about that?' I took her wrists in mine and she pulled away a little. 'Because when I touch you, I don't know whether I want to kiss you or . . . or . . .'

'Kiss me,' she said breathlessly. 'Don't think about the alternative.'

'I can't. If I do, it won't stop there.'

Callie moved closer to me. 'But you saved me. When

your . . . brother lunged for me, you staked him. You staked your own brother. For me.'

'Just in the stomach, not the heart,' I pointed out.

'Still.' She placed her hand on my chest, right over where my heart used to be. I stiffened, trying not to inhale the scent of her.

Before I could react, she pulled a needle out of her pocket and punctured her index finger. I froze.

Blood.

Just one drop of it, like a single ruby, balanced there on the tip of her finger.

God, *Callie's* blood. It smelled like cedarwood and the sweetest wine. My face began to sweat, and my breathing became heavy. My senses sharpened, and my fangs throbbed. Fear flashed in Callie's eyes and radiated off her body.

And just like that, my fangs retracted. I fell backward, panting.

'See, you're not a monster,' she said firmly. 'Not like *he* is.'

The wind picked up, causing Callie's hair to ripple out behind her like the waves in the lake. She shivered, and I stood up, pulling her close.

'Maybe,' I whispered into her ear, drinking in the heady scent of her, my mouth inches from her neck. I couldn't bear to tell her about all the lives I'd taken, how Damon thought that *I* was the monster. 'But he's my brother. And it's my fault he's in there.'

'Do you want me to help you free him?' she said heavily, as if she'd known all along that our conversation would come to this.

'Yes,' I said simply.

Callie chewed on her lip as she played with a strand of her hair, wrapping it on her finger, over and over again.

'But you don't have to.' I avoided her eyes, so I knew I wasn't compelling her.

She stared at me carefully, as if my face were a cipher she could decode.

'In two days,' she said, 'meet me at midnight. That's when Damon will be moved to our attic.'

'Are you sure?'

She nodded. 'Yes.'

'Thank you.' I cupped her cheeks with my hands and leaned forward, pressing my forehead to hers. And then I kissed her.

As we stood, palm to palm, chest to chest, I could have sworn I felt my heart come back to life, beating in perfect sync with hers.

CHAPTER 25

When I got back to the vampire house, the moon was hanging high in the sky. Lexi was sprawled on the sofa, her eyes closed as she listened to Hugo play the piano. The piano was so out of tune that the music he pounded out, which was supposed to be a rousing revolutionary march, sounded more like a funeral dirge. Still, I couldn't help but pull Lexi up, whirling her around in an impromptu dance.

'You're late,' Lexi said, ducking out of the twirl. 'Or were you on another *date*?'

'Or killing more humans?' Buxton asked, entering the room.

'Are you in love?' Percy asked, leaning his elbows on his knees and glancing up at me jealously from the corner table, where he was playing a game of solitaire. Percy clearly loved women, but his childlike face made him look like a boy of fifteen, and often the women he was most attracted to assumed Lexi was his mother. I was thankful I'd been turned into a vampire at the age I had been.

I shook my head. 'I'm *not* in love,' I said, wondering if I was saying it to convince myself. 'But I'm settling into the routine at the freak show. I think I'm learning to like New Orleans.'

'That's great news,' Buxton breathed sarcastically.

'Buxton.' Lexi glanced at him reproachfully before turning her attention back to me. 'Did you forget our plans?'

I racked my brain, but finally shook my head. 'I'm sorry.'

Lexi sighed. 'Remember – I'm taking you shopping. I may be a vampire, but I still have a woman's vanity, and it simply doesn't suit me to be surrounded by men in ill-fitting clothing. What would the neighbours think?' She laughed, amused by her own joke.

'Oh, right.' I inched towards the stairway. 'Maybe we could go tomorrow? I'm exhausted.'

'I'm serious, Stefan,' Lexi said, taking my arm. 'You need clothes, and it's a tradition of sorts. I took those two gentlemen in for fittings, and look at them now,' she said, nodding towards Buxton and Hugo as if exceptionally pleased with her work. It was true. From Buxton's high-collared blue coat to Hugo's well-tailored breeches, they *did* look handsome. 'Besides, you don't have a choice,' she said mischievously.

'I don't?'

'No.' Lexi opened the door with a flourish. 'Boys, we're off. When we come back, you won't even recognize Stefan, he'll look so handsome!'

'Bye, *handsome*!' Buxton yelled sarcastically as the door clicked closed. Lexi shook her head, but I didn't mind. In an odd way, I'd got used to Buxton. He was like a brother of sorts. A brother with a potentially fatal short temper, but one I'd got used to managing.

Together, Lexi and I walked companionably into the cool night air. I saw Lexi looking at me out of the corner of her eye, and I wondered what she saw.

I felt I was living three distinct lives: in one, I was a loyal brother, in another I was a new member of a club I didn't quite understand, and in the third I was a young man placing my trust in a human woman – a woman whom I had staked my own flesh and blood to save. The trouble was, I wasn't sure how to seamlessly live all three lives.

'You're quiet,' Lexi said in midstep. 'And' – she sniffed the air – 'you haven't been drinking human blood. I'm proud of you, Stefan.'

'Thanks,' I murmured. I knew she wouldn't be proud of me if I told her about the conversation Callie and I had shared. She'd say that I was too impulsive, too naïve, that I'd made a huge mistake telling Callie my secret.

Although I hadn't *told* as much as *confirmed* her remarkably accurate suspicions.

'Here we are,' Lexi said, stopping at a nondescript wooden door on Dauphine Street. She took a slim metal hook from her pocket and jiggled it in the lock of the front door. After a moment, it clicked open.

'And now, the shop is open for business.' Lexi spread her hands wide, perching on a stiff leather ottoman. 'Take your pick.'

A dozen mannequins with puffed-out chests held court in the store. One in a tweed jacket lifted its arm in a wave, while another in a sailor's cap had a hand above its eyes, as though staring straight out to sea. Bolts of fine fabrics were propped up against the back wall, and a row of cufflinks glistened under glass. Stacks of ready-made shirts kept silent watch over the darkened shop, and a few cravats spilled out of a drawer.

Lexi crossed her ankles beneath her skirts and gazed at me, a look of pride on her face as I pulled a camel-hair coat off a mannequin and draped it around my shoulders.

I stood stiffly, waiting for approval, as I had done when my mother had taken me shopping.

'Well, I can't tell when you stand there as wooden as a mannequin. Walk around a bit. See what you think,' Lexi said with an impatient wave of her hand.

I rolled my eyes but took a turn around the room, acting like the rich men Callie and I'd seen at the burlesque show. I held out my hand to Lexi with a flourish. 'Care to dance?' I said in an exaggerated British accent.

Lexi shook her head, amusement evident in her eyes.

'OK, I get it. It's a little too dandy. How about that one?' She angled her chin at a mannequin in black trousers and a grey coat with red piping. I removed my jacket and pulled the coat around my shoulders.

Lexi nodded, her eyes taking on a faraway look.

'What are you thinking about?' I asked.

'My brother,' she said.

I thought of the boy in the portrait, his eyes so much like Lexi's. 'What about him?'

Lexi picked up a silk cravat and laced it between her fingers. She didn't look at me as she spoke. 'After our parents died, I started taking walks with a boy who was a vampire. He asked if I wanted to live forever. And of course I did, because I was young, and who *wouldn't* want to always be young and beautiful? Also, if I turned, it meant I'd never have to leave Colin. He'd already lost so much, and I thought, well, at least he could know that he'd never lose me.'

'Was Colin a vampire?'

Lexi pulled the cravat through her fingers and cracked it

like a whip. 'I'd never do that to someone I loved.'

The image of me forcing Damon to drink from Alice, the barmaid in the tavern back home, flashed through my mind. I looked down, not wanting Lexi to sense what I'd done to someone I loved. 'So what happened?'

'People got suspicious. I didn't know then how careful we needed to be. My brother was growing up, and I was staying the same. People wondered. And there was a siege, and our house was torched. And the irony is, I escaped and Colin didn't. And he was the innocent one. He was only sixteen.'

'I'm sorry,' I said finally. I tried to imagine Lexi as a human, leaning on the arm of the man who had promised the world to her, just as Katherine had promised the world to me. I pictured him spiriting her away to a dark alley, taking just a little blood at first, asking her to drink his, then stabbing her through the heart to complete the transformation.

Lexi waved her hand, wiping away the image of herself as a young girl. 'Don't be sorry. It was more than a century ago. He'd be dead anyway by now.' She appraised me. 'That jacket looks good on you.'

'Thank you,' I said. Suddenly the weight of my discussion with Callie felt heavy in my stomach. 'I have a plan to save Damon,' I blurted out.

Lexi's head jerked up, her eyes flashing. 'What?'

'Tomorrow night. Callie's helping me.' I allowed my eyes to meet Lexi's. 'Damon's back at Laurel Street. Her father will be out of the house at a card game, so we'll free Damon then.'

'Did you tell Callie what you are?' she asked, her voice low and hard.

I chewed on my thumb. 'No.'

'Stefan!'

'She guessed,' I said defensively. 'And I trust her.'

'Trust!' Lexi spat. She stood up so abruptly the ottoman toppled over. 'You don't know the meaning of the word. Callie is the daughter of Patrick Gallagher, who just forced your brother to fight a mountain lion to the death. How do you know this isn't some elaborate plan to imprison you, too?'

'How stupid do you think I am?' I challenged, stepping closer to Lexi. 'I may be young, but I have good instincts.'

Lexi gave a derisive snort. 'You mean the same instincts that landed you backed up in a butcher shop with three vampires surrounding you? The same instincts that led you to murder that woman on the train?'

'I'm still here, aren't I?'

'Because of me! And the boys back at the house. But I will not allow you to drag us into confronting Patrick Gallagher, of all people.'

'No one's dragging you into anything!' I yelled in

frustration. 'Just because you let your brother die doesn't mean I'm going to let mine! I owe him that much.'

'You ungrateful child!' she spat, pushing me with all her force against a gold-framed mirror. I fell as the mirror shattered around me. One large shard cut a large gash across my arm, but it barely hurt. Instead, I was shocked by Lexi's strength. I'd seen it before, but I'd never been on the receiving end.

Lexi towered above me, her eyes glittering. 'You need to learn your place, and you need to learn it fast. You're a vampire. And vampires do *not* consort with humans.'

I leaped to my feet and pushed her away from me. She flew across the store and landed against the bolts of fabric.

'This one does, if it means saving Damon,' I growled. Then I stalked out of the shop and into the blackness of the night.

CHAPTER 26

I spent the night at the lake again, but this time I didn't sleep. Instead I sat along the bank, listening to the world hum around me as though I was an audience member at a musical show. Frogs croaked melodically, blowing out their chests with proud puffs. Fish swam to the lake's surface to gulp down the water bugs that hovered there, then dived back down to the depths with soft flips of their tails. Birds flew overhead in V formation, and small animals rustled through the reeds, chasing one another as they ferreted out their next meal.

Then came the grand finale as the sun, an enormous, watery orb, rose to its place of prominence in the sky, signalling that it was the all-powerful king and Earth was its subject.

As I sat there, watching the one thing that could kill me in an instant if it weren't for the ring Katherine gave me, a sense of calm rippled through my body. The world was beautiful and magical and I was lucky to still have a place in it.

Grabbing a perfectly round, flat stone, I stood and looked out over the water. I closed my eyes. *If it skips four times, everything will be OK*. Then I let the stone soar. It skipped once . . . twice . . . three times . . .

'Four skips! Impressive!' a voice cheered, followed by enthusiastic clapping.

I turned around just as Callie leaped into my arms.

'Good morning!' I laughed, spinning her around.

'You're in a good mood,' she said with a smile.

'I am. And it's all thanks to you.'

She tucked her arm through mine. 'In that case, I know just how you can thank me!'

I felt her pulse beating through my coat, and her blood smelled nearly irresistible. But the stone had skipped four times, so I bent down to kiss her.

Callie and I spent all day together, and then I slept at the lake again. When I arrived home the following day at dusk, I found a pile of clothes, including the black trousers and grey coat I'd modelled for Lexi, on the floor outside my room. On top of the pile was a note, written in block handwriting.

Follow your heart. You're lucky you still have one.

I scooped the bundle up into my arms, touched, relieved, and a little bit sad all at once.

I changed into a blue chambray shirt and white trousers and slicked my hair back in the mirror. I looked like any young man preparing for a rendezvous with a pretty girl. I just wished it were that simple.

I crept down the stairs, waiting for someone to jump out of the shadows to stop me – to tell me my plan would never work. But I made it all the way down and then through the kitchen and out the back door without that happening.

Once outside, I walked the two miles to Laurel Street with my hands in my pockets, whistling the strains of 'God Save the South'. I paused to pick a white magnolia from a bush in front of a peach-coloured mansion at the bottom of Callie's street.

'Stefan!' An urgent whisper came from behind the tree at the bottom of the Gallagher driveway.

Callie stepped into view. Her hair was loose and flowing down her back, and she was wearing a white nightdress trimmed in eyelet lace, just like the first time I'd seen her, except that this time she was standing close enough to me that I could see that although she was wearing a heavy grey woollen shawl, she wasn't wearing a petticoat. I turned away, suddenly shy.

'Stefan,' Callie murmured, brushing my arm with her

fingers. 'Are you ready?'

'Yes,' I said. I took the flower and tucked it behind her ear.

She smiled. 'You're such a gentleman.'

'And you're beautiful,' I responded, reaching out to push a strand of hair behind her ear. Her tresses were as soft as rose petals and smelled of honey. I wanted to stay there forever, watching her breath form puffs of air in front of me.

'Callie . . .' I began, when the bells of a distant church chimed suddenly into the frosty air. Twelve bells. Midnight. The witching hour.

'It's time,' Callie said. 'Jasper's shift lasts until twelve thirty, but I can tell him you're there to relieve him early. That will buy us some time. Once the second guard shows up, you'll be long gone. But we have to hurry.' She sounded very sure of herself, but her trembling lip gave away her emotions. I wanted to throw my arms around her, tuck her into bed, and whisper 'sweet dreams' in her ear. But I, a vampire, was relying on this child to protect me.

Callie knitted her fingers together as if in silent prayer. Then she nodded and gave me a wan smile. 'Don't be scared,' she said, pressing her palm into mine. But I could feel her heart thumping at a gallop from the pulse points in her palm.

She led me through the iron gates and around the

gravel driveway, and opened a nondescript door on the side of the house.

'Be quiet,' Callie commanded, as my eyes adjusted to the dark. Unlike the rest of the house, with its polished marble and gleaming oak, this entrance was strictly utilitarian, designed for servants to have easy access to the storage space in the attic without disturbing the residents of the house. A steep staircase, made of unfinished walnut beams, loomed in front of us. Callie cocked her head, listening for something. I followed suit, although my thoughts were buzzing too loudly for me to hear specific words.

Suddenly, I heard a scraping sound from the floor above us. Callie glanced at me; she'd heard it as well.

'Jasper,' Callie explained. 'We should go up.' She walked up the rickety steps, as I followed quickly behind her. Once we got to the cracked, whitewashed door, she knocked – two quick raps followed by a pause, then a longer one.

A lock clicked, and then we heard the scratch of metal against metal as Jasper undid the bolt. Finally, he opened the door, wedging his body next to the edge so we couldn't see inside.

'Well, well, well. Callie and the man who staked the vampire, then ran for his life. To what do we owe the pleasure?' Jasper leered. I shifted uncomfortably, trying to get a glimpse inside the room.

'Hello, Jasper,' Callie said, brushing past him and motioning for me to follow. In the darkness, I could just make out a sizable cage in the corner. A large, unmoving lump lay inside. 'Father needs you in the study. Stefan will take over until the next shift arrives.'

'Meet Jasper in the study?' a loud voice boomed. 'But I'm right here.'

I froze. *Gallagher*.

Callie's father was perched at a rickety table behind the door, a hand of cards laid out in front of him. In the centre of the table, a single candle flickered.

'Oh, Father.' Callie giggled. The sound felt forced, out of place. 'I must have been confused. I know you'd wanted to play cards tonight, and I suppose I thought you'd be more comfortable in the study or . . .' she began, her voice wavering. She licked her lips and sat down at the table across from Gallagher.

'You're kind to think of me, girl,' Gallagher said gruffly.

'Mr Gallagher,' I said, bowing slightly. 'I was told to report for duty, but perhaps I'm mistaken?' The confusion wasn't hard to feign. Callie had sworn her father would be out of the house.

'Is that right, Jasper?' Gallagher asked.

'Guess it is. He ain't bad, that one. A little nervous, but when he sticks 'em, he sticks 'em good.'

Gallagher nodded, taking in the information.

'And this is that boy you trust, Miss Callie?' Gallagher asked his daughter.

Callie nodded, her cheeks reddening under her freckles. Then finally, thankfully, Gallagher stood up, his chair scraping against the floor.

'Well, then, I'll leave you boys to it,' he said, taking his whiskey and following his daughter downstairs.

'So you're Gallagher's guy now, ain't you?' Jasper asked, shoving a vervain-soaked stake in my hands. My skin burned, and pain shot through my arms. I fought the urge to growl and clamped down on my tongue. Tensing, I felt the stake with only two fingers, trying to minimize the contact the poisoned wood had with my body.

'Well, I ain't going to stick around,' Jasper continued. 'The vampire's hungry tonight. Hope he eats you. And while he does that, I'm going to spend some time with Miss Callie and her daddy. Show 'em you're not the only man who can be all friendly and genteel-like,' Jasper said. His movements were loose, and I could smell whiskey on his breath.

As soon as the footfalls faded, I dropped the stake to the ground with an agonized moan, then gingerly walked to the large cage in the corner. Damon was lying in a heap at the corner of the cage like a wounded animal.

'*Brother?*' I whispered.

Damon reared up, fangs bared, causing me to jump back in surprise.

He laughed, a hoarse chuckle, then collapsed against the side of the cage, exhausted from the exertion.

'What, brother? Scared of a vampire?'

I ignored him as I began wresting the door off the structure. Damon watched in curiosity and then slowly crawled over towards me. He was just reaching out when I felt a searing pain radiate from my spine through my entire body.

'Gotcha!' a voice yelled.

The world went weightless, and suddenly I was falling forward. I knocked into something hard – Damon? – and then came the resounding clang of the metal cage door locking behind me.

CHAPTER 27

My heavy-lidded eyes fought to drift open. I didn't know how much time had passed. Was it one night? Two? A week? It was dark, wherever I was. I was vaguely conscious, hearing footfalls and yelling, and once a voice that sounded like Callie's, calling out my name. But one day I woke up without suddenly falling back into unconsciousness. I lifted my arms, realizing I was shackled to the wall. I had vervain burns on my arms and legs. Dried blood crusted my entire body, making it impossible for me to tell where I was wounded. Next to me, Damon was sitting with his knees to his chest. Blood covered his body, and his cheeks were gaunt. Dark shadows rimmed his sunken eyes, but a slow smile was spreading across his face.

'Not so powerful now, are you, brother?'

I struggled to sit up. My bones ached. The attic was soaked in a dim grey light that came from a filthy window.

The padding and sniffing of a mouse sounded somewhere far across the room. It stirred a hunger inside me, and I realized that I hadn't fed since being here. In the corner, two unfamiliar guards were sitting, oblivious to our near-silent conversation.

I shook my head in disgust. How could I have been so stupid? Lexi had been right. Of course she had. Callie had betrayed me. It must have been her plan all along, from the second she'd noticed the ring on my finger that matched Damon's. I should have realized it the moment I'd seen her father in the room. How had I stepped into such a stupid, obvious trap? I deserved to be chained up like an animal.

'Did you love her?' Damon asked, as if he could read my thoughts.

I stared straight ahead.

'She hasn't come to visit, in case you were curious,' Damon continued conversationally. 'She is pretty, though in my humble opinion, you could do better.'

Anger pushed my fangs into place. 'Where are you going with this?' I growled.

Damon gestured to the bars. 'Nowhere, apparently. Excellent job on the rescue attempt.'

'At least I tried,' I said, my fury ebbing and resignation flowing in its place.

'Why even bother?' Damon's eyes flashed. 'Have I not

made my feelings about you perfectly clear?'

'I . . .' I began, before I realized I had no idea where to even start. How could I tell him that rescuing him wasn't a choice? That our blood ran in each other's veins, that we were bound to each other. 'It doesn't matter,' I said.

'No, it doesn't,' Damon said, adopting a philosophical tone. 'After all, we'll both be dead soon enough. The question is, will you be killed by a crocodile or by a tiger? I heard Gallagher saying crocodiles are the best fight opponents, because they don't go for the kill. They drag it out.'

Just then the attic door opened with a flourish, and Gallagher strode into the room, his boots echoing on the floor.

'The vampires are awake!' he bellowed.

The two guards hastily jumped to attention, pretending they'd been watching us the whole time. Gallagher strode towards the cage, kneeling at our eye level. His three-piece suit was impeccable, as if he'd made his fortune as a financier rather than by torturing vampires.

'Well, well, well . . . the family resemblance is obvious. I'm embarrassed to not have noticed it sooner.' He reached through the bars and grabbed the front of my shirt, pulling me against the side of the cage. My face clanged against the bars, and I winced as something wooden jutted into my chest.

A stake.

'And you almost got away with acting like a human!' Gallagher threw his head back and laughed, as if it were the most amusing thing in the world.

'You won't get away with *this*,' I hissed, pain ripping through my body as he dug the stake farther into my skin.

'Pay attention, vampire!' Gallagher said, his lips curled back in a snarl. 'You know, I think I'm going to bet you're the one who'll get killed. Yes, I think that will do very nicely.' He turned towards the two guards. 'Hear that? A tip from the boss. Bet on the dark-haired one,' Gallagher said, twisting the stake against my body. 'I think his brother has more hatred in his belly.'

I couldn't see Damon's face, but I could picture the smirk that no doubt played on his lips.

Gallagher snorted in laughter and threw the vervain-soaked stake to the floor. 'Oh, and I don't want you using the stakes on the vampires for sport anymore,' he said in the direction of the guards. The heavyset one glanced guiltily down at the floor.

'Why not?' the other asked indignantly. 'It's good for 'em. Shows 'em their place.'

'Because we want them in tip-top shape for their fight,' Gallagher said, his voice an exaggerated parody of patience. Then Gallagher smiled at us. 'That's right, boys.

You two are going to be fighting, to the death. It's the perfect solution. I'll have one dead vampire to sell for parts, a live one for performances, and profit beyond my wildest imagination. You know, it might be sacrilege, but I say, thank God for vampires!'

With that, Gallagher turned to leave the attic, slamming the door behind him. I sank back against the bars. Damon did the same, shutting his eyes. The two guards gaped at us through the bars.

'I know the boss said the dark-haired one, there, but ain't he lookin' a little weak? My pennies are goin' for that boy,' one commented.

'Eh, I always go with what the boss says. Besides, ain't all about size, right?' the scrawny one said, sounding affronted by the first guard's implication.

I slumped against the wall, closing my eyes. The hatred that my brother had for me was surely enough to want me dead. But would Damon really kill me?

'I'm more vicious than a crocodile, brother,' Damon said with a smile, his eyes still closed. 'And this is the best piece of news I've heard since we turned into vampires!' He laughed, long and loud, until one of the guards clambered over and, despite Gallagher's decree, jabbed him with a vervain-laced stake.

But even then, he continued to laugh.

CHAPTER 28

'Remember the time we broke Mother's crystal bowl? And I was so worried about how she would react that I cried?' I asked.

'Yes, and then Father decided I was to blame and whipped me and called me wicked,' Damon said dully. 'I tried to make your life easier, little brother. But I'm done. This time, I want you to get exactly what you deserve.'

'What do you want me to say, Damon?' I asked angrily, so loudly the two guards looked up in surprise.

Damon paused, his eyes at half-mast. 'I'll tell you exactly what I want you to say . . . right before I kill you.'

I rolled my eyes in angry frustration. 'I thought you were the one who wanted to die. And now you're going to kill me?'

Damon chuckled. 'You know, now that I think about it, being a beast from hell might not be so bad. In fact, I think it's a role I could take to, immensely. Perhaps it wasn't my newfound state I despised. It was *you*. But if you're gone—'

'If I'm gone you'll be in Patrick Gallagher's freak show forever,' I interrupted.

'But admit it, brother. Don't you think Patrick Gallagher's freak show is more fun than hell? And once I get some strength, I think I can plan an escape quite easily.'

'And then I'm sure you'll get caught, just as you did the first time,' I said in disgust.

I leaned my head back against the cage bars. The fight was one short hour away, and I hadn't given up on trying to engage Damon, to spark any possible thread of connection between us. But no matter what I'd say, he'd taunt me or ignore me.

It was impossible to know just how long we'd been trapped. Since I had become a vampire, time had taken on a different quality. Seconds and minutes no longer mattered. I found being imprisoned gave time back its importance, because every second brought us closer to our battle. As I waited, I played out in my mind the various scenarios the fight could take. I pictured Damon snapping my neck, roaring triumphantly for the crowd. I saw myself succumbing to anger, accidentally stealing life from my brother – again.

But what would happen if we both refused to fight?

Could we take on the entire audience together? Could we somehow engineer an escape? Yes, Gallagher's minions had vervain and stakes, but we had Power. If only I had Callie on my side . . .

My heart panged painfully at the thought of Callie's betrayal. The image of her flame-red hair and gleaming eyes floated to my mind constantly, inflaming my anger – and hurt – over and over. I curled my fists. If only I'd listened to Lexi. If only I hadn't let a human in.

My only goal for the battle was that, if I should die, I would die with my eyes closed, instead of searching the crowd for her face.

'Let's go, boys!' Gallagher called out, pushing open the door as if he were rousing two children for a bright and early hike. He wore a black waistcoat and a brand-new gold watch that glinted in the weak sunlight. He snapped his fingers, and instantly the guards jumped to their feet, bustling to put on the makeshift uniform of a vampire handler: gloves, boots, and vervain-soaked garlands.

The door of the cage flew open, and guards roughly yanked us out, tightened muzzles around our fangs, and shackled our hands behind our backs. We were blindfolded, then marched out of the attic and into the back of a black iron wagon. The wagon took off, bumpily heading down to the lake.

When we arrived at the tent, we were marched in opposite directions.

'Boo!'

'Freak!' I heard the sideshow acts hiss as I was marched through the backstage area. I tightened my jaw. I wondered if Lexi wondered where I was, if she thought I was already dead.

Though I was still blindfolded, I knew every inch of this tent. To the left was the tattooed woman, and to the right was Caroline, the bearded lady. The floor dipped down, and I knew I was in the arena.

I felt something grab my arm. 'I've told a lot of people about what a crafty one you are. But don't try too hard for my benefit, Mr Salvatore. My money is on your brother,' Jasper whispered gleefully.

Finally, the blindfold was removed from my eyes. The tent was lit up like it was midday, and all the stands were crammed with people. At the centre of the ring, Gallagher had set up a betting pool, where people frantically waved bills in the air. Organ music filled the tent, and the air smelled like candied apples and rum punch.

And then, out of the corner of my eye, I saw her.

Callie was weaving through the stands, and behind her was Buck, carrying a tin box. Her hair was plaited with vervain stems, and her face was pale. She'd obviously been dispatched to collect bets in the stand. She was certainly her father's daughter, and she fulfilled her duties well.

She did not look at me once.

I tore my gaze away from her and forced it over to Damon on the opposite side of the ring. Damon had always been a good fighter, and his recent bouts had only strengthened him. If Damon wanted to kill me, he would.

Moreover, I would let him. I owed him that much.

Jasper struck the starting bell, and the crowd hushed. Gallagher stood up from his post in the betting pit and boomed:

'Welcome, ladies and gentlemen, to another fine evening of sport made possible by yours truly, Patrick Gallagher. Only days ago, we brought you the first-ever fight between a vampire and a mountain lion. Tonight, we bring you the first-ever fight between two vampires, including the winner of that previous match. And not only that,' he said, dropping his voice and causing the crowd to hush and lean forward, 'these two monsters are brothers. They came from the same womb, and now one of them will be heading straight to hell.'

A rock hit me in the back of the head, and I whirled around. Vervain was everywhere, causing the sea of faces to blend together in a nightmarish collage of eyes, noses, and open mouths.

'Brother, I'm sorry for anything I've done. Please. If we die,

let's not die in anger. We're all we have,' I whispered, clenching my jaw and trying, one last time, to reach Damon. Damon looked up for a split second and jerked his head, but his expression was unreadable. In the centre of the ring, Gallagher was still commanding the audience's attention.

'The book will be open for another five minutes for final bets. But!—' He raised his hand in the air, attempting to silence the crowd. The noise in the tent dulled, if only slightly. 'Stay after the show, when we'll be selling the loser's blood. Even a dead vampire's blood has healing powers. Cures all ailments. Even ones in the bedroom.' Gallagher winked showily. The crowd catcalled and cheered. I stiffened, wondering whether the crowd thought this was all an act: that we were down-on-our-luck actors and that the blood Gallagher sold after the show would be some type of cherry cordial. Did anyone know that all the blood would be real, that the fallen loser in the centre of the ring wouldn't be standing up and heading home once the tent was emptied?

Callie knew. Callie knew, and she had decided that this would be my fate. I again clenched my jaw, ready to fight, ready to give the audience the show it was looking for. Suddenly, I found myself being led around the ring by Jasper, giving the audience one final chance to scrutinize my strength before raising their stakes. I could hear snatches of conversation from all sides of the tent:

That one's got an inch on the other. I'm swapping sides.

How'd your old lady like one of those for your anniversary?

I wonder how they'd do against a real lion.

A man dressed in clerical robes stood next to Gallagher, raising his frocked arms to quiet the crowd. I recognized him as the snake charmer from the sideshow.

'May all good light shine upon this fight and return the loser's soul to the cleansing fires of hell!' he yelled, causing the tent to erupt in a cacophony of noise. A whistle blew, and the fight was on.

Damon circled towards me, his stance low to the ground, like when we were kids and practised boxing. I imitated his stance.

'Blood!' one drunken man yelled, practically hanging over the railing of the ring.

'Blood! Blood! Blood!' The entire tent seemed to be cheering. Damon and I continued to circle each other.

'*Let's not do this*,' I said. '*Let's refuse. What can they do?*'

'*We're beyond that, brother*,' Damon said. '*The two of us can't survive in the same world*.'

Anger seeped into my limbs from the centre of my being. Why couldn't we? And why couldn't Damon forgive me? I no longer thought he was haunted by the memory of Katherine. Instead, I believed he was haunted by *me*. Not who I was, but who he thought I was – a monster who killed without fear or awareness of consequence. How dare he not even recognize the lengths I'd gone to to try to make him happy, to try to save him? I swung, connecting with Damon's cheek. Blood spurted under his eye, and the crowd roared.

Damon wound up and swung back, hitting me on my shoulder and knocking me down to the ground.

'*Why did you do that?*' Damon hissed, baring his teeth to the delight of the crowd.

'*Because you wanted it*,' I hissed back, baring my own teeth, then flipped him over into a headlock.

He freed himself quickly and returned to his corner. We stood at opposite sides of the ring, staring at each other, both confused, angry, alone.

'Fight!' the crowd roared again. Gallagher glared at us, unsure what to do. He snapped his fingers, and Jasper and Buck ran towards us with stakes, determined to force us to fight each other. They prodded us until our bodies were only inches apart and both of our fists were raised, when a huge, echoing, booming crack that sounded like the sky splitting in two echoed from above. A cold wind whipped around us, causing a cloud of sawdust and debris to rise at our feet. I smelled smoke.

'Fire!' a panicked voice yelled.

I looked around wildly. Part of the tent was on fire, and people were running in all directions.

'Come on!'

I felt hands shoving my shoulders. Callie. My eyes opened wide in surprise. '*Go, go, go!*' Callie yelled, pushing me. She held an axe in her hand, and slowly I began piecing together what had happened. Had she actually cut down the supports of the tent structure, then set the fire?

'Move!' Callie pushed me one more time. She was surprisingly strong for a human, and after a few seconds of stupidly standing and blinking in place, I grabbed Damon by the wrist, and we ran, past the tents, away from the river, faster and faster, heading towards my home.

CHAPTER 29

Damon and I ran at vampire speed through the streets of New Orleans. Unlike when we first arrived and Damon lagged reluctantly behind me, we ran side by side, the adobe and brick houses blurring past us like melting wax.

Something had shifted between us in that arena, I felt it in my very being. Something had changed in Damon's eyes as he'd regarded me and refused to attack, even as the crowd jeered on. I wondered how the match would have ended had the tent not gone up in flames – would we have taken the humans one by one, or would one Salvatore brother have ended up dead and bloodied on the dusty floor?

The image of the Mystic Falls church blazing like an oversize torch sprang to my mind. The town had burned down the church and the vampires trapped within it the night our father killed us – and the vampire Damon had loved.

But Damon and I were still here, like phoenixes rising from the ashes of the vampires who came before us. Perhaps out of the fire of this circus in our new home city, a new kinship between us would spring to life – like the new life that arose in prairies after the previous year's crops had been burned to the level of the soil.

Damon and I continued to run, our feet slapping against the cobblestones in perfect unison, down the back alleys and streets I'd learned so well in my few weeks of living here. But as we rounded the corner onto Dauphine, the same street where Lexi had taken me shopping, I stopped short. Affixed to the window of the tailor's shop was a crude drawing of me and Damon, our fangs bared, both of us crouched low. *The fight of the century*, the posters read. I wondered if Callie had drawn them. Probably.

Damon leaned in close, examining the poster. 'That drawing makes you look a bit stocky, brother. Might be time to lay off the barmaids.'

'Ha, ha,' I said dryly, looking around. Shouts sounded behind us, in the direction of the circus. We had a good head start, but if Callie had distributed these posters as widely as we had the posters for Damon, then we wouldn't be safe until we were inside.

The spindly spire of a church rose in the distance – the church that was kitty-corner to Lexi's place.

'Come on!' I pushed Damon in the direction of the church, and we didn't talk until we reached the rickety white house.

'This is where you live?' Damon's lip curled as his eyes flicked up from the sagging, whitewashed porch to the dark windows.

'Well, I understand that it may not measure up to your standards, but we all must make sacrifices every now and again,' I said sarcastically as I led him to the back door.

The door swung open, allowing a triangular slice of light to pour out over the dark backyard.

I put my hands up as Lexi appeared in the doorway. 'I know you said no visitors, but—'

'Come in. Quickly!' she said, locking the door the second we crossed the threshold. In the main room, candles were burning, and Buxton, Hugo and Percy were all perched on the chairs and couches, as if they were in the middle of a meeting.

'You must be Damon.' Lexi nodded to him slightly. 'Welcome to our home.' I was aware of Damon watching her, and wondered what he saw.

'Yes, ma'am,' Damon said with an easy grin. 'And I'm afraid that during our time in captivity, my brother somehow failed to mention you and your' – his eyes flicked over Percy and Buxton – 'family.'

Percy bristled and half-rose from his seat, but Lexi put up a hand to stop him. 'I'm Lexi. And as Stefan is your brother, my home is your home.'

'We escaped,' I started to explain.

Lexi nodded. 'I know. Buxton was there.'

'You were?' I whirled around in surprise. 'Were you betting for me or against me?' Damon let out a little snort.

Lexi laid a hand on my forearm. 'Be nice. He was there to help you.'

My eyes widened. 'You were going to help me?'

Buxton leaned back in his chair. 'I was. But then someone had the bright idea to burn down the whole place, so I left.' He crossed his arms over his chest, looking pleased at himself for being part of the action.

'It was Callie. She lit the fire,' I said.

Lexi's eyes registered surprise. 'I was wrong,' she said simply. 'It's been known to happen.'

'You must forgive my poor manners in interrupting, but do you have anything to eat?' Damon asked, not turning away from the portrait of an old woman that he was examining. 'I've had a rather difficult few weeks.'

For the first time since we had escaped, I really looked at my brother. His voice was hoarse, as if he was unused to using it. Bloody gashes covered his arms and legs; his clothes were in tattered rags; and his shock of black hair was filthy and lank against his pale neck. Red rimmed his eyes, and his hands trembled slightly.

'Of course. You boys must be starving.' Lexi tsked. 'Buxton, take him to the butcher shop. Let him eat his fill. I doubt there are enough humans in New Orleans to quench his thirst. And tonight, at least, he deserves to eat like a king.'

'Yes, ma'am,' Buxton said, bowing slightly as he raised his bulk from the chair.

'I'll join him,' I said, heading towards the door.

'No.' Lexi shook her head and grabbed my arm – hard. 'I have tea for you.'

'But . . .' I protested, confused and annoyed. I could practically taste the pig's blood on my tongue.

'No buts,' Lexi said sharply, sounding remarkably like my mother.

Buxton opened the door for Damon, who wiggled his brow at me as if to say, 'Poor boy!'

If Lexi saw, she pretended not to notice, instead busying herself with the tea kettle while I slumped on one of the rickety chairs set up around the table, my head resting on my hands.

'When you become a vampire, it's not just your teeth and diet that change,' Lexi said as she stoked the fire in the stove, her back towards me.

'What does that mean?' I asked defensively.

'It means that you and your brother aren't who you used to be. You've both changed, and you may not know Damon as well as you think,' Lexi said, carrying two steaming mugs in her hands. 'Goat's blood.'

'I don't *like* goat's blood,' I said, pushing the mug away angrily. I sounded like a petulant toddler, and I didn't care. 'And no one knows Damon better than I do.'

'Oh, Stefan,' Lexi said, looking at me kindly. 'I know. But promise me you'll be careful. These are dangerous times – for everyone.'

At the word *dangerous*, something clicked in my mind. 'Callie! I have to find her!'

'No!' Lexi pushed me back down on my chair. 'Her father will not harm her, but he'll kill you, given half the chance, and you're in no shape for a fight.'

I opened my mouth to protest, but Lexi cut me off.

'Callie is fine. You can see her tomorrow. But for now, drink the blood. Fall asleep. When you awaken, you will be healed, and you, Damon and Callie will figure out everything then.'

Lexi left the kitchen with a swish of her aprons and extinguished the lamp.

Suddenly exhaustion fell over me like a heavy blanket, and the desire to fight Lexi's advice drained from my body. With a sigh, I lifted the mug and took a small sip. The liquid was warm and velvety, and I couldn't help but admit that it was good.

Lexi was right – I would see Callie tomorrow to say goodbye. But I needed rest. My entire body hurt, even my heart.

At least you know you have one, I imagined Lexi saying, and I smiled in the darkness.

CHAPTER 30

October 19, 1864

I'm out of danger, but I don't feel safe. I wonder if I'll ever feel safe again, or will I forever long for a desire that I'll never fulfil? Will I get used to the ache? Twenty, two hundred, two thousand years from now, will I even remember these weeks? And will I remember Callie and her red hair, her laugh?

I will. I have to. Callie has saved me and given me another chance at life. In a way, it's like she was the daylight that followed the darkness Katherine had cast upon my existence. Katherine turned me into a monster, but Callie has changed me back into the Stefan Salvatore I'm proud to be.

I wish her love. I want nothing but the best for her. I want for her to live in the light and find a man – a human

– who will appreciate and adore her, who will take her away from Gallagher's house forever to a quiet home on a lake, where she can teach her children to skip stones.

Maybe that's how I'll live in her memory: not as a monster, but simply as someone who shared a warm summer morning with her and taught her that skipping stones was as simple as a flick of the wrist. Maybe someday we'll both be thinking of that memory at the same time. Maybe she'll even tell her children, and her children's children, and they will all know me as the man who taught her to skip stones. It is a tiny hope, but it is something. Because as long as Callie remembers me, then she and I are somehow connected. And maybe, in time, simply being connected by a single strand of remembrance will be enough.

I woke in the middle of the night to what I thought were hailstones bouncing against the windowpane. Despite Lexi's rules, I peeked through a tiny slit in the curtains and squinted into the darkness. The trees were bare, their branches like ghostly limbs stretching towards the sky. Though it was a moonless night, I could see a raccoon scamper through the yard. And then, a figure standing timidly behind one of the columns on the portico.

Callie.

I hastily pulled on a shirt and slipped down the stairs, taking care to not make any noise. The last thing I wanted was for Buxton or Lexi to know that a human had followed me home.

The door shut with a thud behind me, and I saw Callie jump.

'I'm here,' I whispered, feeling thrilled, confused, and excited, all at once.

'Hi,' she said shyly. She was wearing a blue dress and a fur stole. A hat was pulled low over her curls, and she had a large carpetbag over her shoulder. She nodded, shivering. I wished more than anything that I could bring her upstairs so we could lie under my covers and warm up.

'Are you going somewhere?' I asked, nodding at her bag.

'I hope so.' She clasped my hands with her own. 'Stefan, I don't care what you are. I've never cared. And I want to be with you.' She looked into my eyes. 'I . . . I love you.'

I gazed at the ground, a lump in my throat. Back when I was a human, I thought I'd loved Katherine until I saw her, chained up, muzzled, and foaming at the mouth. I'd felt nothing but disgust at that vision. And yet Callie had seen me unconscious, bleeding from vervain, staked by captors, and pummelling my brother in the ring, and she still loved me. How was that possible?

'You don't have to respond,' Callie rushed on. 'I just had

to tell you. And I'm leaving no matter what. I can't stay here with Father, not after everything that's happened. I'm getting on the train, and you can come with me. But you don't have to. But I want you to,' she babbled.

'Callie!' I interrupted, placing a finger to her lips. Her eyes widened, shifting between fear and hope.

'I would go with you anywhere,' I said. 'I love you, too, and I will for the rest of my life.'

Callie's face broke into a relaxed, joyful expression. 'You mean your un-life,' she said, her eyes dancing.

'How did you know where I lived?' I asked, suddenly shy.

Callie blushed. 'I followed you home once. When you ran away after the first vampire fight. I wanted to know everything about you.'

'Well, now you do.'

Unable to restrain myself, I pulled her into my arms and lowered my lips to hers, no longer afraid to hear the blood coursing in her veins or to hear her heart beat faster in anticipation. She tightened her grip around me, and our lips touched. I hungrily kissed her, feeling the softness of her lips against mine. My fangs didn't grow, my desire was all for her, in her human form, as she was.

She was soft and warm and tasted like tangerines. In those moments, I imagined our future. We'd take the train as far away from New Orleans as possible, maybe to California, or perhaps even sail to Europe. We'd nest in a little cottage and keep livestock for me to feed from, and Callie and I would live out our days together, away from the prying eyes of society.

A nagging thought tugged at the corner of my mind: would I turn her? I hated the thought of doing it, of sinking my teeth into her white neck, of making her live a life in which she craved blood and feared the daylight, but I also couldn't bear the thought of seeing her grow old and die in front of me. I shook my head, trying to release those thoughts. I could deal with them later. We both could.

'Stefan,' Callie murmured, but then the murmur turned into a gasp, and she slipped out of my clutches and onto the ground. A butcher's knife stuck into her back, blood pooling out of it.

'Callie!' I cried, sinking to my knees. 'Callie!'

Frantic, I tore a vein in my wrist, trying to feed Callie my blood to heal her. But before I could press my arm to her gasping mouth, an unseen hand yanked me up by the shirt collar.

A low, familiar chuckle cut through the night air. 'Not so fast, brother.'

CHAPTER 31

I whirled around, my hand ready to strike, my fangs bared. Before I could move, Damon grabbed my shoulders and flung me across the street. My body hit the road, hard, my arm snapping at an unnatural angle. I scrambled to my feet. Callie was lying in the grass, her red hair fanning over her shoulder, a pool of blood darkening around her. She let out a quiet moan, and I knew she must be in agony.

I started to race back to her, pumping my blood to my open wound so she could feed easily. But Damon intercepted me, lowering his shoulder into my chest and knocking me backward.

I scrambled to my feet. 'This stops now!' I yelled, ready to pounce. I flew towards him, ready to rip him apart, to give him what he'd wanted for so long.

'Does it stop now? Before dinner?' Damon asked, a slow smile forming on his face. I watched in horror as Damon knelt down, bared his teeth, and sank them into Callie's neck, drinking long and hard. I tried to push him away, but he was far too strong. How many people had he fed from since our escape?

I kept tugging, trying to free Callie, but Damon stayed in the same position as if he were a marble sculpture.

'Help! Lexi!' I roared, as Damon sent me flying backward with a swift jab of his elbow.

I hit the grass with a thud. Damon kept drinking. I realized with horror that Callie's moaning had stopped. So had the steady, thrumming sound of blood I'd got so used to hearing in Callie's presence. I fell to my knees.

Damon turned towards me, his face smeared with blood. Callie's blood. I blanched at the sight. Damon chuckled. 'You were right, brother. Killing is what vampires do. Thanks for the lesson.'

'I'll kill you,' I said, rushing towards him once more. I knocked him to the ground, but Damon took advantage of my injured arm and flipped me over, pinning me to the ground next to Callie.

Damon shook his head. 'I don't think I will die tonight, thank you. You're done being the one to make the life-and-death decisions,' he hissed.

He stood up, as if he were going to walk away. I crawled over to Callie. Her eyes were wide open and glassy, her face pale. Her chest was still rising and falling, but barely.

Please live, I thought, gazing into her unblinking eyes in a desperate attempt to compel her. I saw her eyelids flutter. Could it be possible that it was working?

I want you to live. I want to love you while you're alive, I thought, squeezing blood from my wounds into her open mouth.

Then, as drops fell on her face, I felt an agonizing pain in my abdomen. I sprawled on the grass as Damon kicked me over and over and over in the stomach, a demonic look in his eye.

Summoning all my strength, I scuttled on the dew-damp earth away from Damon.

'Help me,' I called again towards the house.

'Help me!' Damon mocked in a singsong voice. 'Not quite the big man, anymore, are we, little brother? What happened to taking over the world? Got too busy having tea parties with your little friends and falling in love with humans?' He shook his head in disgust.

Something inside me snapped. Somehow, I pushed myself to my feet and raced towards Damon, fangs bared. I pushed him to the ground, my fangs carving a long, jagged cut along his jugular vein. He fell to the ground, blood draining from his neck, his eyes closing.

For a moment, he looked like my brother again. No

bloodshot eyes, no voice laced with hatred. Just the broad shoulders and dark hair that always symbolized Damon. And yet he wasn't Damon anymore. He was a monster on a spree of destruction, stopping at nothing to make his threat of making my life miserable come true.

I surveyed the ground around us, finally glimpsing a small tree limb, a few feet away, fallen after a storm. I crawled over to the branch and raised it high above his chest.

'*Go to hell*,' I whispered, fervently meaning each word.

But as the words left my mouth, Damon lunged up from the ground, his eyes red and his fangs bared. 'That's no way to talk to family,' he scoffed, throwing me to the ground. 'And that's no way to hold a stake.'

He raised the branch high over my chest, a gleam in his eye.

'Here's the death you didn't let me have. Slow, and painful, and I'm going to enjoy every second of it,' Damon said, cackling as he brought the stake down with all his might against my chest.

And then everything went black.

CHAPTER 32

'Stefan,' a disembodied voice whispered.

I was in the labyrinth back at Veritas, the lush green hedges rising higher than my head, the sun beating down upon my shoulders. My collar was itchy and constrictive – for some reason I was in my Sunday best.

From around the bend Damon approached, his blue eyes wide and innocent. 'Want to race, brother?' he challenged.

Of course I accepted.

We ran until we gasped for breath, our lungs spent from exertion and laughter. Damon smiled at me happily, until a cloud shifted and everything went dark. To my horror, his features morphed and changed. His eyes darkened, and his lips became as red as blood. The next thing I knew, he was upon me, tackling me to the ground, but not in play. He reached for something in his pocket, and then he struck me in the chest, and I lay there on the soft grass, gasping my last breath.

Suddenly, we were sitting on the porch swing, with Katherine wedged between us, mischief in her dark eyes, as she plucked petals from a daisy. Her leg was so close I felt it grazing mine. As her gaze shifted back and forth, I realized the game she was playing: the flower would determine which one of us she would choose. When she reached the final petal, her eyes locked onto mine, and I knew that I was the victor. She leaned in to kiss me, and I closed my eyes, anticipating the soft touch of her lips.

But instead I felt a stake plunge into my heart. My eyes fluttered open, and there stood my brother, laughing as he dug the wood yet deeper into me, the flower petals crushed beneath my prone form.

My head lolled to the side, and my eyes snagged on the girl who was bleeding to death next to me on the grass. Her hair was fire-red, and her skin was moon-pale beneath her freckles.

Callie! I tried to shout. But Damon snatched up my words in his fist before sinking a knife over and over into Callie's back.

'Stefan!' a voice called again, louder this time. I recognized the lilting alto. *Lexi*.

'Nooo . . .' I moaned. I couldn't allow Damon to kill her, too. 'Go away!'

'Stefan . . .' She came closer still, kneeling down beside

me, holding a goblet to my lips.

'No,' I said again.

She shook my shoulders violently. My eyes popped open. The walls around me were painted with cracked red paint, and I saw a gilt-edged portrait on the opposite wall. I sat up, touching my face with my hands, then glancing down. I was still wearing my ring. I touched the stone. It felt very real.

'Lexi?' I asked thickly.

'Yes!' She smiled, clearly relieved. 'You're awake.'

I glanced down at my body. My arm still throbbed, and there was dried blood underneath my fingernails. 'Am I alive?'

She nodded. 'Just barely.'

'Damon?'

'We didn't get him,' Lexi said darkly. 'He ran off.'

'Callie?' I asked. I didn't want to hear, but I needed to know.

Lexi looked down at her fingernails for a long moment, then lifted her amber eyes to mine. 'I'm sorry, Stefan. We tried . . . even Buxton tried to save her . . .'

'But she was too far gone,' I finished for her. My head throbbed. 'Where is she now?'

Lexi pushed my matted hair off my temple. Her fingers were cool against my burning skin. 'In the river. The whole city's looking for her . . .' Lexi's voice trailed off, but I understood everything that she wasn't saying.

The entire freak show knew of my friendship with Callie. So if people were looking, my presence was a danger to Lexi and her family.

But even if my days here weren't numbered, I wouldn't be able to stay. New Orleans contained too much hurt and too many memories, ones that I hadn't even begun to process.

I flopped back against my pillows.

'Before you rest, you need to drink,' Lexi murmured, helping me sit up again. 'It's your favourite, pig's blood,' she said with a sad smile.

I put my lips to the goblet. The brackish liquid tasted nothing like sweet, full-bodied human blood, but it was warm. And it contained something human blood never would: a dull spark of redemption. The more of this I drank, the less human blood would run through me.

I wasn't naïve, though. Guilt would always flow through my veins. I'd killed too many in my short time as a vampire, destroyed too many lives. Whether or not I drank from her, Callie's death was on my hands as well. I should have turned my back on her, told her I never wanted to see her. But I'd been weak.

'Good boy,' Lexi murmured as I finished drinking from the cup.

I didn't feel good. I felt sick and scared and unsure of

what to do. Damon was still out in the world, somewhere, and Callie's blood was running through his veins. My stomach tightened.

'I don't know what to do,' I admitted, searching Lexi's eyes for answers. But Lexi was silent.

'I don't know what to tell you,' she said finally. 'But I do know you're a good man.'

I sighed, ready to point out that I wasn't a man at all, I was a monster. But Lexi stood up and gathered the mugs from the night table.

'No more talking. Rest,' she said, pressing her lips to my forehead. 'And try, my dear Stefan, not to dream.'

CHAPTER 33

When I woke up, I could tell from the light streaming through the crack in the curtains that it was daylight. I swung my feet onto the hardwood floor and grabbed the neat pile of clothes from the shopping trip with Lexi. It seemed like a lifetime ago.

I put on a new shirt, slicked my hair back, and put the rest of the clothes in a makeshift carrying case formed from my tattered shirt from Mystic Falls – the only item I still had from my old life.

I glanced around the room, my eyes taking in the familiar layers of dust in the corners. I wondered how many vampires had passed through this house and whether Lexi would find another young vampire to take under her wing. I hoped, for his sake as well as hers, that he'd have a better time in this city of sin than I had had.

Lexi was sitting in the living room. In her hands was

the portrait of her brother. As soon as I stepped in, she glanced up.

'Stefan,' she said.

'I'm sorry,' I cut in. And I was, for all of it. For coming to New Orleans. For disrupting her life. For bringing danger to the tiny spot of security the vampires had managed to carve out.

'I'm not. It was a privilege to have you.' Her gaze turned serious. 'I'm sorry about Callie – and about your brother.'

'He's not my brother anymore,' I said quickly.

Lexi set down the portrait on the coffee table. 'Perhaps not anymore. But as you said yourself, he was for your whole human life. Can you remember that and forget the rest?'

I shrugged. I didn't want to remember Damon. Not now, not ever.

Lexi crossed the room and put her hand on my arm. 'Stefan, missing humans and your human life hurts. But it does get easier.'

'When?' I asked, my voice cracking slightly.

She glanced back at the portrait on the table. 'I'm not sure. It happens gradually.' She paused, then laughed, the sound so innocent and lighthearted that I wanted to sit down and stay at the house forever. 'Let me guess. You want it to happen now.'

I smiled. 'You know me well.'

Lexi frowned. 'You need to learn to slow down, Stefan. You have an eternity ahead of you.'

A silence fell between us, the word *eternity* clanging in my ears.

With a jerk, I pulled Lexi into a hug, inhaled the comforting aroma of our friendship, then sped out of the house without a glance back.

Once outside, I chastised myself for my sentimentality. I had much to atone for, and feeling sorry for myself was self-indulgent. I paused at the spot on the street where Callie had died. There was no bloodstain, nothing to mark the fact that she'd even existed. I knelt down, glancing over my shoulder before I kissed the pavement.

Then I stood up and began to run, faster and faster. It was dawn, and the city was just waking up. Messenger boys zipped by on delivery bikes, and Union soldiers marched through the streets, their rifles nestled in their arms like infants. Vendors were already setting up on the sidewalk, and the air smelled like sugar and smoke.

And, of course, like the tangy scent of blood and iron.

I quickly reached the train station, where the platform was already bustling. Men in morning coats sat on worn wooden benches in the waiting area, reading newspapers, while women nervously clutched their purses. The entire station had an air of festive transience. It was the perfect hunting ground. And before I could help it, my fangs protruded from my gums.

Bowing my face into my hands, I counted to ten, fighting the hunger that raced through me and waiting for my teeth to click back into their human form.

Finally, I joined a wave of people who were headed to the platform and took a spot at the far end. Next to me, two lovers were entwined in an embrace. A soldier ran his hand through the woman's strawberry-blonde hair, and the woman, balancing on her tiptoes, held on to his shoulders as if she never wanted to let go.

I watched them for a long moment, wondering if in a different life Callie and I could have played out that same scene. If she would have kissed me as I went off to battle, then waited eagerly on the platform for my return home.

The whistle blew, and the train roared into the station, kicking up a cloud of dust and breaking me out of my reverie.

I followed the soldier on board, wondering if he and his lover would experience a happy ending. I took solace in knowing, at least, that should they not, it would not be because of me.

I entered the coach compartment.

'Ticket, sir?' a conductor asked, holding out his hand.

I locked eyes with him, my stomach turning with disgust

at having to rely on my Power.

Let me pass. 'I showed it to you,' I said aloud. 'You must have forgotten.'

The conductor nodded, stepping aside to allow me on. The train lurched out of the station, taking me to a new life. One where I would never compel unless I had to, and one where I'd never again taste human blood.

EPILOGUE

Once I stopped drinking human blood, I became even better at hearing a heartbeat, knowing in an instant, from the speed of a pulse, whether a human was sad or annoyed or in love. Not that I was around humans very much. After I left New Orleans, I truly was a creature of the night, sleeping during the day and venturing into the outside world only when humans were safe in their beds, fast asleep. But occasionally I'd hear a quickening heartbeat and know that someone was climbing from a window or sneaking out a door to meet a lover, stealing a few moments of intimacy.

That was the hardest sound to hear. Whenever I did hear it, I was reminded of Callie, of her fluttering heart and quick smile. Of how alive she was, and how she was not afraid to be in love with me despite my true nature. Now, when I think of our plan to escape, I can't help but laugh bitterly at myself for ever thinking it could have been a possibility. It had been the same foolish mistake I'd made when I'd fallen in love with Katherine, believing that humans and vampires could love each other, that our differences were just a minor detail that could be easily solved. But I wouldn't fall into that trap a third time. Whenever vampires and humans dared to love each other, death and destruction were sure to follow. And I had enough blood on my hands to last an eternity.

I would never know the extent of the harm Damon was causing in the world. Sometimes I'd see a newspaper article or hear snatches of conversation about a mysterious death, and my mind would instantly jump to my brother. I'd listen for him, too, always waiting to hear him call 'Brother' in his exaggerated drawl.

But mostly I listened to myself. The longer I subsisted on animal blood, killing the odd squirrel or fox in a forest, the more my Power ebbed, until it was simply a faded thrum in the background of my being. Without Power, I lost the electric sense of feeling alive, but the guilt I would carry for the rest of my existence had dulled around the edges. It was a trade-off, one of many I'd learned to make, and one of many more I'd have to make in the eternity that stretched in front of me.

So I made the vow to always keep moving, to never stay in one place too long or grow too close to anyone. That is the only way I'll do no harm. Because God help us all if I ever fall in love with another human . . .

WANT MORE OF
STEFAN'S DIARIES?

TURN THE PAGE FOR
A SNEAK PEEK AT
THE CRAVING,

PREFACE

Everything has changed. My body, my desires, my needs, my appetite.

My soul.

In seventeen short years, I've borne witness to more tragedy than anyone should – and been the cause of far too much of it. With me I carry the memory of my death, and that of my brother. The sound of our last breaths in the mossy woods of Mystic Falls, Virginia, haunts me. I see my father's lifeless body on the floor of his study in our magnificent Veritas Estate. I still smell the charred church where the town's vampires burned. And I can almost taste the blood I took and the lives I stole out of sheer hunger and indifference after my transformation. Most clearly I see the curious dreamer of a boy I once was, and if my heart could beat, it would break for the vile creature I've become.

But though the very molecules of my being have morphed beyond recognition, the world continues to turn. Children grow older, their plump faces thinning with the passage of time. Young lovers exchange secret smiles as they chat about the weather. Parents sleep while the moon keeps watch, wake when the sun's rays nudge them out of slumber, eat, labour, love. And always, their hearts pump with rhythmic thuds, steady, loud, hypnotic, the blood as alluring to me as a snake charmer's tune is to a cobra.

I once scoffed at the tediousness of human life, believing the Power I had made me more. Through her example, my maker, Katherine, taught me that since time holds no sway over vampires, I could become divorced from it, living from moment to moment, moving from one carnal pleasure to the next with no fear of consequences.

But now the strength I have is a burden, the constant thirst for blood a curse, the promise of immortality a terrible cross to bear.

Before I left New Orleans, I battled the monster my brother, Damon, had become – a monster I had a hand in creating. Now, as I remake myself up North, far from anyone who's ever known me as either a human or a vampire, the only demon I have to battle is my own hunger.

CHAPTER 1

I picked out a heartbeat, a single life, in the near distance.

The other noises of the city faded into the background as this one called to me. She had wandered from her friends and left the well-worn paths.

The sun had set over Central Park, where I'd exiled myself since arriving in New York seven long days ago. The colours in this expanse of wilderness were softening, sliding towards each other, shadows blurring with the things that made them. The oranges and deep blues of the sky morphed into an inky black, while the muddy ground dimmed to a velvety sienna.

Around me, most of the world was still, paused in the breath that comes at the end of the day when the watches change: humans and their daylight companions lock their doors and the creatures of the night like myself come out to hunt.

The heartbeat I pursued now began to recede, its owner moving away. Desperate, I took off, forcing my body to move quickly, my feet to push off from the ground. I was weak from lack of feeding and needed every spare bit of energy for the hunt. I crashed through bushes and trees, my chase growing far louder than I intended. My hunting skills had weakened along with my strength.

The bearer of the heart I followed heard and knew her death was close behind her. Now she was entirely alone, cut off from her crowd, and aware of her plight. She began to run in earnest.

What a spectacle I must have made: dark hair askew, skin as pale as a corpse's, eyes starting to redden as the vampire in me came out. Running and leaping through the woods like a wild man, still dressed in the finery Lexi, my friend in New Orleans, had given me, the white silk shirt now torn at the sleeves.

She picked up speed. But I wasn't going to lose her.

My need for blood became an ache so strong that I could contain myself no longer. A sweet pain bloomed along my jaw and I felt my fangs come out. The blood in my face grew hot as I underwent the change. My senses expanded as my Power took over, sapping my last bit of vampiric strength.

I leaped, moving at a speed beyond human and animal. From rock to low branch I raced towards my prey, closing the distance between us in mere seconds. With that instinct all living creatures have, the poor thing felt death closing in and began to panic, scrambling for safety under the trees. Her heart pounded out of control: thump-*thump* thump-*thump* thump-*thump*.

The tiny part of me that was still human might have felt bad for what I was about to do, but the vampire in me needed the blood.

With a final jump, I caught my prey – a large, greedy squirrel who'd left her pack to scavenge for extra food. Time slowed down to a standstill as I descended, ripped her neck aside, and sank my teeth into her flesh, draining her life into me.

I'd eaten squirrels as a human, which lessened my guilt marginally. Back home in Mystic Falls, my brother and I used to hunt in the tangled woods that surrounded our estate. Though squirrels were poor eating for most of the year, they were fat and tasted like nuts in the fall. Squirrel blood, however, was no such feast; it was rank and seared my tongue. Still, I forced myself to keep drinking.

It was nourishment, nothing more – and barely that. It was a tease, a reminder of the fresh, thick sweet liquid that runs in a human's veins.

It had only been one month since a vampire named Katherine had transformed me into a creature like her, but

I'd crowded that time with too much horror and tragedy. Heady with my new Power, the limitless strength and speed of a vampire, I tore through humans as if their lives were meaningless. Every warm drop made me feel alive, strong, fearless and powerful.

Even concentrating, trying to send myself back mentally to see the faces of each of my victims, all of those people I killed, I couldn't. Except for one:

Callie.

Her flame-red hair, her clear green eyes, the softness of her cheeks, the way she stood with her hands on her hips . . . every detail of her stood out in my memory with a painful clarity.

It had been Damon, my brother and former best friend, who had dealt Callie her final blow, but her death weighed heavily on my conscience. Callie had made me feel human again. She made me remember what it was to have a normal life, and what it meant to value that life. And she had died because of me, because Damon hated me for turning him into a vampire. I had taken his life, so he took from me the only thing he could: my new love.

From that moment on, I swore off humans forever. I would never kill another human, never feed from another human, and never love another human. I could only bring them pain and death, even if I didn't mean to. That's what life as a vampire meant. That's what life with Damon as my brother meant.

An owl hooted in the elm that towered over my head. A chipmunk skittered past my feet. A branch broke somewhere nearby. My shoulders slumped. I had taken my fill this evening and ended one innocent life. Now it was time for me to move on.

I laid the poor squirrel down on the ground. So little blood remained in its body that the wound didn't leak, the animal's legs already growing stiff with rigor mortis. Then I wiped the traces of blood and fur from my face and headed deeper into the park, alone with my thoughts, while a city of nearly a million people buzzed around me.

Since I'd snuck off the train at Grand Central Depot a week earlier, I'd been sleeping in the middle of the park in what was essentially a cave. I'd taken to marking a concrete slab with the passing of each day. Otherwise moments blended together, meaningless, empty, and never, ever ending. Next to the cave was a fenced-in area where construction men had gathered the 'useful' remains of a village they had razed to make Central Park, as well as the architectural bric-a-brac they intended to install: carved fountains, baseless statues, lintels, thresholds, and even gravestones.

Just as I pushed past a barren branch – November's chill

had robbed nearly every tree of its leaves – the teasing, cloying scent of rust and iron drifted past my nose.

Instantly I became the hunter again: balanced on my toes, fingers flexing, ready to claw. All my senses became even more aroused: eyes widened to capture every shadow, nostrils flared to gather in the smells. Even my skin prickled, ready to detect the slightest change in air movement, in heat, in the minute pulses that indicated *life*.

There it was again. A painful, metallic tang. The smell of blood. *Human* blood.

I stepped into the clearing, my breath coming rapidly. The thick stench of blood was everywhere, filling the hollow with an almost palpable fog. I scanned the area. There was the cave where I spent my tortured nights, tossing and turning and waiting for dawn. There was the spider's jumble of beams and doors stolen from knocked-down houses and desecrated graves. There were the glowing white statues and fountains to be installed around the park.

And there, thrown at the base of a statue of a regal prince, was the body of a young woman, her white ball gown slowly turning a bloody red.

CHAPTER 2

My eyes narrowed, and I felt the veins in my face crackle with Power. My fangs came out quickly and violently, painfully ripping through my gums.

The girl was small, but not sickly or dainty. She looked to be about sixteen. Her flesh was firm and her bosom, barely moving as she grew weaker, was full. Her hair was dark, with curls highlighted in gold by the light of the rising moon. She had been wearing silk flowers and ribbons in her hair, but these, along with her tresses, had come undone, and trailed out behind her head like sea foam.

Her dress had a dark red slip underneath with frothy white cotton tulle that floated on top. Where her petticoats were torn, slashes of scarlet silk showed through, matching the blood that was seeping out of her chest and down her bodice. One of her doeskin gloves was white, the other nearly black with soaked blood, as if she had tried to stanch her wound before she'd passed out.

Thick, curly lashes fluttered as her eyes rolled beneath their lids. This was a girl who clung to life, who was fighting as hard as she could to stay awake and survive the violence that had befallen her.

My ears, finer tuned than the best hound's, could easily make out her heartbeat. Despite the girl's strength and will, it was slowing. I could count seconds between each beat.

Thud . . .

Thud . . .

Thud . . .

Thud . . .

The rest of the world was silent as a grave: just me, and the moon, and the racket of life this dying girl made. Her chest stopped rising. She would most likely be dead in mere moments, and not by my hands.

I had done my best. I had hunted down a squirrel – a *squirrel* – to sate my appetite. I was doing everything I could to resist the lure of the dark side, the hunger that had been slowly destroying me from within. I had refrained from using my Power.

But the smell . . .

Spicy, rusty, sweet. It made my head spin and caused the world to come together in a flash of red and pink.

It wasn't my fault she had been attacked. It wasn't I who

had caused the pool of blood to form around her prone body. Just one little sip couldn't hurt . . . I couldn't hurt her any more than she already was . . .

I shivered, a delicious pain fluttering up my spine and down my body. My muscles flexed and relaxed of their own accord. There it was, the luscious liquid of life. I took a step closer, so close that I could reach out and touch the red substance.

Human blood would do far more than sustain me. It would fill me with warmth, with Power, with purpose. Nothing tasted like human blood, and nothing *felt* like it. Just a mouthful and I would be back to my old New Orleans self: invincible, lightning-fast, strong . . . powerful. I'd be able to compel humans to do my bidding. I'd be able to drink away my guilt and embrace my darkness. I'd be a real vampire again.

In that moment, I forgot everything: why I was in New York, what happened in New Orleans, why I left Mystic Falls. Callie, Katherine, Damon . . . all were lost, and I was drawn wordlessly, mindlessly, to the source.

I knelt down in the grass. My parched lips drew back from my mouth, fangs fully exposed.

One lick. One drop. One taste. I needed it so badly. And technically, I wouldn't be killing her. *Technically*, she would die because of someone else.

Her heart slowed even more. Narrow streams of blood ebbed and flowed down her chest, pulsing with her heart. I leaned over, my tongue reaching forward . . . One of her eyes fluttered open weakly, her thick lashes parting to reveal clear green eyes, eyes the colour of clover and grass.

The same colour eyes Callie had.

In my last memory of her, Callie was lying on the ground, dying, in the same helpless pose. Callie also died of a knife wound – but in her back. Damon didn't even have the decency to let her defend herself. He stabbed her while she was distracted, telling me how much she loved me. And then, before I could feed her my own blood and save her, Damon threw me aside and drained her completely. He left her a dry, dead husk and then tried to kill me, too. Had it not been for Lexi, he would have succeeded.

With a scream of agony, I pulled my hands back from the girl and pounded the ground. I forced the bloodlust that was in my eyes and cheeks back down to the dark place from which they came. I resisted the Power, the night, and my hunger.

I took a moment longer to compose myself, then pulled the girl's bodice aside to view her wound. She had been stabbed with a knife, or some other small and sharp blade. It had been shoved with near perfect precision between her breasts and into her rib cage – but had missed her heart. It was as though the attacker had *wanted* her to suffer, to slowly bleed out rather than die immediately.

I grabbed a sharp rock to slice open my wrist. It was difficult and not very effective, but I pushed hard. The pain helped to focus me, a good, clean pain compared to that of my fangs coming out.

With incredible effort I pushed my wrist to her mouth and squeezed my fist. I had so little blood to spare as it was – this would nearly kill me. I had no idea if it would even work, since my Powers had declined with feeding just on animals.

Thump-*thump*.

Pause.

Thump-*thump*.

Pause.

Her heart continued to slow.

'Come on,' I pleaded through teeth gritted in pain. '*Come on*.'

The first few drops of blood hit her lips. She winced, stirring slightly. Her mouth parted, desperate.

With all my strength, I squeezed my wrist, literally pushing the blood out of my vein and into her mouth. When it finally hit her tongue she almost gagged.

'Drink,' I ordered. 'It will help. *Drink*.'

She turned her head. 'No,' she mumbled.

Ignoring her feeble protests, I shoved my wrist against her mouth, forcing the blood into her.

She gave a little moan, still trying not to swallow.

And then she stopped fighting.

Her lips closed down on the wound in my wrist, and her soft tongue sought out the source of my blood. She began to suck.

Thump-*thump*.

Thump*thump*.

Thump thump thump.

Her heartbeat quickened.

Her hand, the one in the blood-soaked glove, came fluttering up weakly and grasped my arm, trying to draw it closer to her face. She wanted more. I understood, but I had no more to offer her.

'That's enough,' I said, feeling faint myself. I gently disengaged my arm despite her mewling cries. Her heart was beating more regularly now.

'Who are you? Where do you live?' I asked.

She whimpered and clung to me.

'Open your eyes,' I ordered.

She did, once again revealing her Callie-green eyes.

'*Tell me where you live*,' I compelled her, using the very last remaining drops of my Power.

'Fifth Avenue,' she answered dreamily.

I tried not to grow impatient. '*And what? Fifth Avenue and what?*'

'Seventy-third Street . . . One East Seventy-third Street . . .' she whispered.

I scooped her up, a perfumed confection of silk and gauze and lace and warm, human flesh. Her curls brushed my face, tickling across my cheek and neck. Her eyes were still closed and she hung limply in my arms. Blood, either hers or mine, dripped down into the dust, threatening to drive me mad again.

I gritted my teeth and began to run.

If you liked *Stefan's Diaries* you'll be dying to sink your teeth into *Night World* by the same bestelling author.

Here's a taster for you . . .

CHAPTER

1

It was on the first day of summer vacation that Poppy found out she was going to die.

It happened on Monday, the first *real* day of vacation (the weekend didn't count). Poppy woke up feeling gloriously weightless and thought, No school. Sunlight was streaming in the window, turning the sheer hangings around her bed filmy gold. Poppy pushed them aside and jumped out of bed – and winced.

Ouch. That pain in her stomach again. Sort of a gnawing, as if something were eating its way toward her back. It helped a little if she bent over.

No, Poppy thought. I refuse to be sick during summer vacation. I *refuse*. A little power of positive thinking is what's needed here.

Grimly, doubled over – think positive, idiot! – she made her way down the hall to the turquoise- and gold-tiled bathroom. At first she thought she was going to throw up, but then the pain eased as suddenly as it had come. Poppy straightened and regarded her tousled reflection triumphantly.

'Stick with me, kid, and you'll be fine,' she whispered

to it, and gave a conspiratorial wink. Then she leaned forward, seeing her own green eyes narrow in suspicion. There on her nose were four freckles. Four and a half, if she were completely honest, which Poppy North usually was. How childish, how – *cute*! Poppy stuck her tongue out at herself and then turned away with great dignity, without bothering to comb the wild coppery curls that clustered over her head.

She maintained the dignity until she got to the kitchen, where Phillip, her twin brother, was eating Special K. Then she narrowed her eyes again, this time at him. It was bad enough to be small, slight, and curly-haired – to look, in fact, as much like an elf as anything she'd ever seen sitting on a buttercup in a children's picture book – but to have a twin who was tall, Viking-blond, and classically handsome . . . well, that just showed a certain deliberate malice in the makeup of the universe, didn't it?

'Hello, Phillip,' she said in a voice heavy with menace.

Phillip, who was used to his sister's moods, was unimpressed. He lifted his gaze from the comic section of the *L.A. Times* for a moment. Poppy had to admit that he had nice eyes: questing green eyes with very dark lashes. They were the only thing the twins had in common.

'Hi,' Phillip said flatly, and went back to the comics. Not many kids Poppy knew read the newspaper, but that was Phil all over. Like Poppy, he'd been a junior at El Camino High last year, and unlike Poppy, he'd made straight As while starring on the football team, the hockey team, and the baseball team. Also serving as class president. One of Poppy's greatest joys in life was teasing him. She thought he was too strait–laced.

Just now she giggled and shrugged, giving up the menacing look. 'Where's Cliff and Mom?' Cliff Hilgard was their stepfather of three years and even straighter-laced than Phil.

'Cliff's at work. Mom's getting dressed. You'd better eat something or she'll get on your case.'

'Yeah, yeah . . .' Poppy went on tiptoe to rummage through a cupboard. Finding a box of Frosted Flakes, she thrust a hand in and delicately pulled out one flake. She ate it dry.

It wasn't *all* bad being short and elfin. She did a few dance steps to the refrigerator, shaking the cereal box in rhythm.

'I'm a . . . sex pixie!' she sang, giving it a foot-stomping rhythm.

'No, you're not,' Phillip said with devastating calm. 'And why don't you put some clothes on?'

Holding the refrigerator door open, Poppy looked down at herself. She was wearing the oversize T-shirt she'd slept in. It covered her like a minidress. 'This *is* clothes,' she said serenely, taking a Diet Coke from the fridge.

There was a knock at the kitchen door. Poppy saw who it was through the screen.

'Hi, James! C'mon in.'

James Rasmussen came in, taking off his wrap-around Ray-Bans. Looking at him, Poppy felt a pang – as always. It didn't matter that she had seen him every day, practically, for the past ten years. She still felt a quick sharp throb in her chest, somewhere between sweetness and pain, when first confronted with him every morning.

It wasn't just his outlaw good looks, which always reminded her vaguely of James Dean. He had silky light brown hair, a subtle, intelligent face, and grey eyes that were alternately intense and cool. He was the handsomest boy at El Camino High, but that wasn't it, that wasn't what Poppy responded to. It was something *inside* him, something mysterious and compelling and always just out of reach. It made her heart beat fast and her skin tingle.

Phillip felt differently. As soon as James came in, he stiffened and his face went cold. Electric dislike flashed between the two boys.

Then James smiled faintly, as if Phillip's reaction amused him. 'Hi.'

'Hi,' Phil said, not thawing in the least. Poppy had the strong sense that he'd like to bundle her up and rush her out of the room. Phillip always overdid the protective-brother bit when James was around. 'So how's Jacklyn and Michaela?' he added nastily.

James considered. 'Well, I don't really know.'

'You don't *know*? Oh, yeah, you always drop your girlfriends just before summer vacation. Leaves you free to manoeuvre, right?'

'Of course,' James said blandly. He smiled.

Phillip glared at him with unabashed hatred.

Poppy, for her part, was seized by joy. Goodbye, Jacklyn; goodbye Michaela. Goodbye to Jacklyn's elegant long legs and Michaela's amazing pneumatic chest. This was going to be a wonderful summer.

Many people thought Poppy and James's relationship platonic. This wasn't true. Poppy had known for years that she was going to marry him. It was one of her two great ambitions, the other being to see the world. She just hadn't gotten around to informing James yet. Right now he still thought he liked long-legged girls with salon fingernails and Italian pumps.

'Is that a new CD?' she said, to distract him from his stare out with his future brother-in-law.

James hefted it. 'It's the new Ethnotechno release.'

Poppy cheered. 'More Tuva throat singers – I can't wait. Let's go listen to it.' But just then her mother walked in. Poppy's mother was cool, blond, and perfect, like an Alfred Hitchcock heroine. She normally wore an expression of effortless efficiency. Poppy, heading out of the kitchen, nearly ran into her.

'Sorry – morning!'

'Hold on a minute,' Poppy's mother said, getting hold of Poppy by the back of her T-shirt. 'Good morning, Phil; good morning, James,' she added. Phil said good morning and James nodded, ironically polite.

'Has everybody had breakfast?' Poppy's mother asked, and when the boys said they had, she looked at her daughter. 'And what about you?' she asked, gazing into Poppy's face.

Poppy rattled the Frosted Flakes box and her mother winced. 'Why don't you at least put milk on them?'

'Better this way,' Poppy said firmly, but when her mother gave her a little push toward the refrigerator, she went and got a carton of low fat milk.

'What are you planning to do with your first day of freedom?' her mother said, glancing from James to Poppy.

'Oh, I don't know.' Poppy looked at James. 'Listen to some music; maybe go up to the hills? Or drive to the beach?'

'Whatever you want,' James said. 'We've got all summer.'

The summer stretched out in front of Poppy, hot and golden and resplendent. It smelled like pool chlorine and sea salt; it felt like warm grass under her back. Three whole months, she thought. That's forever. Three months is forever.

It was strange that she was actually thinking this when it happened.

'We could check out the new shops at the Village—' she was beginning, when suddenly the pain struck and her breath caught in her throat.

It was bad – a deep, twisting burst of agony that made her double over. The milk carton flew from her fingers and everything went grey.

the Vampire Diaries
The Awakening & The Struggle
Elena Gilbert is used to getting what she wants and she wants mysterious new boy, Stefan. But Stefan is hiding a deadly secret – a secret that will change Elena's life for ever …
itv 2 Now a major itv2 series
the Vampire Diaries
The Awakening & The Struggle
L. J. SMITH
itv 2 Now a major itv2 series

the Vampire Diaries
The Fury & The Reunion
Faced with an ancient evil, Stefan and Damon must stop their feuding and join forces with Elena to confront it. But in so doing, they are unwittingly sealing her fate ...
Now a major itv2 series
the Vampire Diaries
L. J. SMITH
itv 2
Now a major itv2 series

Now a major itv2 series
the Vampire Diaries
The Return – Nightfall
L. J. SMITH

NIGHT WORLD

Volume 1
Books 1-3
OUT NOW

Secret Vampire

Poppy is dying, and it seems that James is her only chance of survival … but is the price too high?

Daughters of Darkness

Mary Lynette has just met three mysterious sisters – on the run from their cruel brother. But can she protect them or herself with another threat lurking nearby?

Enchantress

Blaise is irresistible … and deadly, but the Night World has rules, and Blaise is breaking them all …